Evaluating Educational Software

By

Carol A. Doll

AMERICAN LIBRARY ASSOCIATION

Chicago and London 1987

Designed by Charles Bozett

Composed by Precision Typographers
in Baskerville on a Quadex/
Compugraphic 8400 typesetting
system

Printed on 50-pound Glatfelter, a
pH-neutral stock, and bound in
10-point Carolina cover stock by
Thomson-Shore, Inc.

Library of Congress Cataloging-in-Publication Data

Doll, Carol Ann, 1949–
    Evaluating educational software.

    Bibliography: p.
    1. Computer-assisted instruction—Evaluation.
2. Education—Computer programs—Evaluation.   I. Title.
LB1028.5.D65   1987   370'.28'5536   87-1417
ISBN 0-8389-0474-2

Contents

1

Educational Microcomputer Software and the School

Because of recent technological advances, microcomputers are compact, powerful, and inexpensive, especially when compared to their predecessors. As a result, microcomputers are being used in government, businesses, homes, and schools. The number and types of microcomputers, applications for microcomputers, and microcomputer software are still increasing.

The microcomputer and its software are being integrated into the educational process with increasing frequency, and are especially important in the areas of computer literacy, classroom management, and direct involvement with student instruction. The focus of this book will be on the selection and evaluation of quality software programs designed to enhance and support classroom learning. Such programs may include sections to record student scores and similar data—but software that is primarily designed to calculate student grades, maintain attendance records, and perform other classroom management tasks will *not* be considered. Nor will this book concentrate on materials designed to increase student knowledge of microcomputers or on ability to use them. While this kind of literacy may indeed be the topic of an educational software program (also evaluated by the teacher or media specialist), computer literacy itself will not be the main topic.

Teachers and media specialists instruct students in many different ways. Information can be presented to large groups, small groups, or individuals. Books, other print materials, and audiovisual items can be used to provide visual, aural, and tactile experiences. Microcomputers and microcomputer software can now be added to the array of materials available. They can be used, with large screen monitors, to present information or demonstrations to an entire class. Small groups or individuals can work more independently.

Microcomputers and their accompanying software are used in the classroom and media center with increasing frequency to assist instruction. With appropriate software, it is possible to use the microcomputer to help teach any subject at any age, grade, or developmental level. The determining factors should be the quality of software and the agreement between program contents and classroom objectives.

Drill and practice programs are appropriate when students need additional work with material they should memorize. The letters of the alphabet, beginning math facts, state capitals, foreign-language vocabulary, or chemical symbols may all be appropriate topics for a drill and practice program.

Tutorial software is designed to present some new information and then generally gives the user a chance to apply or practice the information or skills discussed. Again, the type of program can be appropriate for many topics on many levels of difficulty: alphabetization, card catalog skills, or techniques for taking the SAT.

Microcomputer games can reinforce instruction and give students a chance to apply information and skills learned earlier. Software games are available on beginning graphing skills, on reinforcing and developing logical thinking for fourth and fifth graders, or on allowing high school students to plan strategy.

Microcomputers can be particularly effective in simulations, which re-create the essential elements of a situation and use student input to determine subsequent actions and reactions. Elementary students can "follow" the Oregon Trail while older students can "run" the Three Mile Island nuclear reactor or "perform" physics experiments.

Drill and practice programs, tutorials, games, and simulations can all be used very effectively in an instructional situation. It is the responsibility of the teacher or media specialist to evaluate the quality and content of a particular program to identify those which are truly appropriate for a particular class or individual students.

There are two main advantages to the increasing use and availability of instructional microcomputer software. First, children and young adults learn in different ways. Some learn best when information is presented visually, but others prefer oral instruction; some need tactile stimulation, while a combination of several methods is most effective for others. With this diversity of learning styles, educators should use several types of media for instruction, such as books, films, and recordings. Microcomputer software is another source of information or instruction which can help broaden the learning environment, and therefore it is important.

Second, microcomputers and their software have the potential to facilitate individualized instruction. A well-written, individually paced program can provide the appropriate amounts of instruction and problems, presenting new information only when the student is ready. Slow students are not pressured and fast learners are allowed to proceed as soon as they have mastered the current portion of the program. Educators rarely have enough time to give each student this type of individual attention; so microcomputers are important for this reason, too.

While microcomputers can be and probably will become even more valuable to education, they only assist in the instructional process. They are one tool, albeit a powerful one, which can be used to help present information or develop skills. The teacher or school library media specialist is, and will continue to be, indispensable. The trained education professional is the one who has the expertise needed to design, select, execute, and evaluate a learning experience. These professionals have the skills needed to diagnose student learning problems, then match the software to specific learner needs. They can also evaluate the student's progress and level of knowledge, as well as develop a total package of classroom learning experiences and foster an atmosphere which encourages thinking and learning. It takes the flexibility and judgment in a human brain and heart to orchestrate and control these types of activities. No microcomputer can replace the teacher or school library media specialist in this respect.

Microcomputers and microcomputer software are incapable of independent thinking. They can do only what they are told to do. They cannot draw inferences, reach a conclusion, or make a value judgment. Instead, these machines and their programs are totally inflexible. Because of this, it is vital that high-quality software be selected for use in school, so that the instructions to the microcomputer support the educational process and help students learn.

Both school library media specialists and teachers should be involved in the selection process. Teachers have been trained in selecting and using materials in classroom instruction which support and promote learning. Teachers select items to meet the needs of students in their classrooms. Films, filmstrips, television programs, audiorecordings, and realia have been among the media chosen to help students understand and learn the concepts, ideas, and skills presented.

To a certain extent, the school library media specialists are involved with materials with individual users, but their responsibilities extend beyond that particular task. *Media Programs: District and School* charges media professionals with building and maintaining an adequate collection to support the total instructional program of the school. These standards were published in 1975, before microcomputers and microcomputer software were as commonly used for instruction as they are today. Educational microcomputer software is not mentioned in the 1975 standards

3

as an information format for which school library media specialists should be responsible. However, they are charged with building a quality collection through the selection and evaluation of books, periodicals, pamphlets, newspapers, models, realia, maps, globes, films, filmstrips, slides, pictures, audiorecordings, video tapes, and various graphic formats. Decisions on the acquisition and/or use of an item, regardless of format, should be based on an informed evaluation of the content and technical aspects of the item and on the needs of the individual school and students.

Furthermore, school library media specialists also are charged with instructional design responsibilities. This involves working with classroom teachers to help them become more aware of materials, including microcomputer software, which are available in and through the media center. The school library media specialists should also be able to work with teachers to develop strategies and techniques for using these items in the teaching process.

Educational microcomputer software should be accepted as another form of informational media and treated in the same manner. The same rigorous evaluation criteria that are used to select a library's books and audiovisual materials and to identify items for classroom use must also be applied to microcomputer software.

Although not the panacea that some educators originally believed, the microcomputer, together with good educational software, can be a powerful tool and an effective supplement to classroom instruction. School library media specialists and teachers need to be aware of the full range of possibilities for microcomputers in education. They can and should develop the skills needed to identify educational software programs which will enable students to make the best use of microcomputers.

The following chapters offer school library media specialists and educators specific elements to consider when evaluating educational microcomputer software. A procedure is suggested for determining whether or not a program is suitable for purchase or use. They will build on basic evaluation skills that media specialists and teachers already possess, but will add the often missing specific criteria for microcomputer software.

SELECTED SOURCES

American Library Association. American Association of School Librarians, and Association for Educational Communications and Technology. *Media Programs: District and School.* Chicago: American Library Assn., 1975.

Harper, Dennis O., and James H. Stewart, eds. *Run: Computer Education* (2nd ed.). Monterey, Calif.: Brooks/Cole, 1986.

Kepner, Henry S., ed. *Computers in the Classroom.* Washington, D.C.: National Education Assn., 1982.

Kleiman, Glenn M. *Brave New Schools: How Computers Can Change Education.* Reston, Va.: Reston Publishing Co., 1984.

Watt, Molly. ''Making a Case for Software Evaluation,'' *Computing Teacher* 10 (May 1982): 20–22.

2
Presentation of Content

When teachers and school library media specialists select books and other materials to use with students in an educational setting, they judge the quality of the information presented in these items. The same types of standards should also be applied to educational microcomputer software.

Quality of the information presented should not, of course, be the only criterion used to judge educational software. A program may be so complicated that users become confused or discouraged. Efficient use of the microcomputer's strengths, an overall design which promotes learning, and good interaction with students are among other factors to be considered in a balanced evaluation. These factors will be explored later in this book; meanwhile, this chapter will identify and discuss specific areas concerned with the quality of information in educational software.

Accuracy

The content of the software program *must* be correct. That is, the information *must* be error free and accurate. Dinosaurs should not breathe fire at little men with horns growing from their heads. Bismarck is the capital of *North* Dakota, not South Dakota. Fortunately, mistakes like these are decreasing in frequency, compared to materials produced several years ago.

Occasionally a program will contain spelling mistakes or grammatical errors—probably the result of poor editing or hasty production. Such programs, of course, should not be used with students. Educators need to check all programs selected to use in the school and must avoid purchasing or using those with mistakes or inaccuracies.

Currency

The information in the software program should be up to date or current, although the importance of this criterion depends, to a certain extent, on the subject matter. The rules and concepts of arithmetic or mathematics rarely change. The "facts of history" also change infrequently, although their interpretation changes from time to time. Current events and topics, such as the space program in the United States, change rather rapidly. The teacher or school library media specialist should evaluate the content of a software program in terms of its currency.

Balance

Information in an educational microcomputer software program should be presented in a logical and objective manner. The content should be factual and there should not be any bias. Instead, both sides of issues or several points of view should be presented. If an author or producer chooses to emphasize one point of view, other opinions should be acknowledged in a nonjudgmental manner.

Furthermore, there should not be evidence of stereotyping. Instead, when women, minorities, the elderly, and other groups are a part of the program, they should be presented in a realistic manner. When there is an opportunity, women and minorities can also be presented in a nontraditional way, as when "the doctor" is portrayed as a woman.

Appearance of the Information

In addition to general content, educators should check the manner in which material is presented on the computer screen or the order in which students must type in their answers. (A detailed discussion of the application of computer capabilities in educational software is presented in Chapter Six.) In some cases, the method of presentation or student response can affect the content of the program. For example, when addition, subtraction, or multiplication are performed with paper and pencil, answers are written from right to left. In some arithmetic programs, however, students' answers can only be entered (i.e., put into the computer) from the left to right of the computer screen. That is, a student must first type 2, instead of 8, after adding 13 and 15. A software program that accepts answers only in this way could confuse young learners. Since it conflicts with the way their calculations are done, it requires students to work a problem by hand and have the complete answer before putting any numbers into the computer—which can defeat the purpose of computer instruction.

Sometimes, only uppercase letters are used to show information on the computer screen. This is not always a problem, but occasionally beginning readers and primary students are confused by this approach.

Educators should be aware of potential difficulties which could be caused by the way information is presented on the computer screen and must determine whether or not they would confuse students.

Program Compatibility

The program and its content should be compatible with other materials and textbooks in the school. If the program refers to two main parts of a sentence as the subject and predicate, textbooks in the English classroom should use the same terminology. If the math textbooks teach long division one way:

$$
\begin{array}{r}
61, \ r5 \\
7\overline{)432} \\
\underline{42} \\
12 \\
\underline{7} \\
5
\end{array}
$$

there could be confusion if the program teaches an alternative method:

$$
\begin{array}{r|l}
7\overline{)432} & 20 \\
\underline{140} & \\
292 & 40 \\
\underline{280} & \\
12 & 1 \\
\underline{7} & \\
5 & 61
\end{array}
$$

In general, terminology, procedures, symbols, and information in educational software should not conflict with these categories in other media.

Summary

Microcomputer software programs should be

    A. Accurate and error free
    B. Up to date or current
    C. Unbiased and free of stereotypes

D. Presented on the computer screen in a nonconfusing manner
E. Compatible with texts and other materials

SELECTED SOURCES

Bland, Barbara B. "Evaluation: The Key to Selecting Quality Microcomputer Courseware for School Media Collections," *North Carolina Libraries* 40 (Fall/Winter 1982): 191–97 + .

Gallagher, Francine L. "What Educators Want in Microcomputer Software," *Catholic Library World* 55 (February 1984) 290–93.

MicroSIFT. *Evaluator's Guide for Microcomputer-Based Instructional Packages.* Eugene: Dept. of Computer and Information Science, Univ. of Oregon, 1982.

3

Educational Quality

When designing a lesson plan or other learning experience, education professionals follow certain procedures that promote student learning. Teachers and school library media specialists study for years to learn strategies for planning classroom activities. These strategies include procedures and criteria used to select specific materials for classroom or educational use. Numerous books and journals explore and evaluate many different teaching techniques and materials (generally in more depth and detail than in this chapter). However, there are specific elements for which educators can check in microcomputer software when evaluating the educational quality of programs.

Production Concerns

Certain things can be done during the creation and production of software programs which can enhance the educational quality of the final product. Evidence that these areas were addressed can be found either in the *documentation* (written materials that accompany the program) or on the disk itself.

The author (or authors) of a program can be quite important to its instructional effectiveness. When microcomputers were first becoming available in schools, the demand for software was high but the supply was low. In fact, some authors of this early software were computer programmers who had little or no background in education. The result was technically good programs that were inappropriate for classroom or school library media center use. It is usually beneficial if the authors or producers of a program have a background or training in education.

It is also important to check for evidence that the program was pretested and then revised in response to information gathered during this initial run. That is, the software should be used with children and/or young adults *before* it is widely distributed. Information that is gathered during this type of controlled use allows the programmers to identify problems or mistakes in the program and then to change or correct them. Some producers regularly submit their products to this type of analysis. Materials which accompany the disk may indicate if, how, and when such pretesting was done; or the absence of mistakes and a well-presented program may imply that an initial testing procedure was followed. While absolute evidence of pretesting is not mandatory, it can be an indication of better-quality software.

In any teaching situation, goals and objectives are specified and used to guide the development of the lesson or lessons. The goals and objectives of lessons that are presented in software should, moreover, be identifiable. Program objectives should accurately reflect the content of the software and meet a variety of student ability levels. There is evidence that students learn better when they are told in advance what they are expected to learn. Education should not be a guessing game. A formal, explicit statement of behavioral objectives is not necessarily required, but the teacher or school library media specialist should be able to identify program objectives and ensure that students will be aware of these objectives.

If goals and objectives are not given, the program should be very well organized and its content presented clearly. Then the teacher or school media specialist can easily determine what the program intends to teach, whether quadratic equations or the letters of the alphabet.

Furthermore, the program will probably be used to help teach or reinforce some fact, concept, or skill. Therefore, the objectives of the program should match, to some extent, the pertinent objectives of the classroom. In this way the software can enhance, supplement, and support school activities, instead of just filling in time and supplying student busywork.

Information Presentation

When examining the content of the program, the evaluator should watch for evidence of sound educational practice. For example, the material should be presented in small, well-sequenced units. When a skill or concept is taught, the best approach is usually to identify the subunits of information which, when presented in the proper order, allow students to understand and assimilate the material.

Primary students are not initially given the rules for addition in their entirety. Instead, objects are manipulated, sums less than 10 are pre-

11

sented, then multidigit numbers, then carrying, and so on, until the entire concept of addition has been carefully and sequentially presented. The same technique should be the basis for educational software programs. Learning becomes more difficult, or even impossible, when poorly constructed materials can confuse students.

A good educational program gives more than one opportunity to master the skills or information presented. A *branching* program (discussed in Chapter Six) can be flexible enough to provide additional material or practice for students who need it and can advance students who are ready for the next lesson. Learning does not always occur instantaneously. In fact, only rarely is information or a skill mastered at one stroke. Teachers and school library media specialists are aware of this and build repetition into student activities. Educators should also look for repetition in educational microcomputer software.

Wherever possible, the information in the program should use or build on the familiar and known to explain the new and unknown. For example, students will probably develop a better understanding of metric volume if the discussion centers on quantities of milk sold in stores and filling the car's gas tank, instead of concentrating on graduated cylinders. Students should be well versed in English grammar (e.g., direct and indirect objects or subjunctive verb tenses) before dealing with these concepts in Spanish. A microcomputer program which builds on known information is likely to be more effective than one which does not.

Furthermore, to enhance and promote learning, the student response required by the program should be directly related to the skill being emphasized. Three types of user responses are used in educational software: recognition, recollection, and application. For recognition, students are presented with a list or selection of possible answers and asked to identify the correct one. That is, they need only recognize the right answer when it is placed in front of them. The difficulty of this task depends on the material covered, the quality of the wrong choices, and the amount of thinking or calculation required of the student to select the correct response. This technique tends to be popular in educational software, and it is relatively easy to program this activity.

When the task is recollection, a question is posed to the student, who must then supply the correct answer. This works for software only where there is one answer or a limited number of answers to the question. The software then compares the user response to the correct answer or answers to determine whether or not the student is right. This technique is valid with material the student should memorize and which is unambiguous and limited. Number facts, spelling, and naming state capitals are some of the items students are asked to remember. (This recollection technique is different from recognition, in which the student is given "clues" to the answer. Instead, the student must independently remember the answer or be able to calculate it from a set of memorized rules. Recollection, where the student is on his own, can be somewhat more difficult than recognition, in which the student knows the right answer is on the list.)

Finally, some software asks the students to apply or practice the skills they already have, in a new situation. For example, student knowledge of nuclear reactors is used to prevent meltdown at Three Mile Island. Or mapping skills, recordkeeping, and reading are among the skills used by students as they gather clues to identify the culprit in *Snooper Troops* software. This type of program tends to concentrate less on facts and to encourage students to think. The skills needed to operate this type of program tend to be more advanced than those for recognition or recollection.

Each of these techniques can be valid at different times and in different programs, and can be used for all subject areas. When evaluating software, educators should determine whether or not the type of response required of the user truly matches both the objectives of the program and the objectives of the teacher or the school media specialist. For example, if the program is designed to teach spelling, students should be required to type in the entire word and then be evaluated on that performance. Programs which ask students to identify correctly spelled words from a list presented on the screen are *not* teaching spelling. Instead, they are teaching the recognition of correctly spelled words, which *can* be an appropriate area for instruction. But spelling a word correctly and identifying a misspelled word are two different skills and should have two different types of responses in microcomputer programs.

When evaluating or selecting educational software, educators first need to identify the type of learning they expect to occur. That is, will the students need to recognize, recollect, or apply knowledge or skills? Then the software itself must be examined to determine whether user responses are based on recognition, recollection, or application. There should be an appropriate match between the type of response required by the program and the type of learning the teacher or the school media specialist wants to occur. Only then will that program be both effective and appropriate for classroom or media center use.

Software should not offer evidence which directs students to the correct answers. In quickly or carelessly written items, the right response may be the only one where the subject, given in the question, matches the predicate, given in one of the possible answers. Or words that are highlighted may always be the desired responses in the questions which follow. Students are intelligent enough to detect such patterns and follow them, instead of fully participating in the program.

Matching the Intended Audience

Every educational software program should identify its target audience by age, grade, or desired level of acquired skills. Based on this information, programs can be examined to determine whether their content matches the intellectual or developmental level of the target audience.

Some learner characteristics depend on the developmental level or chronological age of the learner. As a child grows, his attention span increases. A four-year-old user may have an attention span of five to ten minutes. By age eleven, a student can concentrate for up to forty minutes. This means that software for younger children should move more quickly and finish sooner than programs designed for older students.

Frustration level is another element which varies with age. Any user can become frustrated with a microcomputer and its program, but young users will reach the point at which they can no longer work with an unwieldy program sooner than older students.

Furthermore, evaluators need to consider the microcomputer and how it works in selecting appropriate programs. Software is precise, and is both structured and limited by the demands of rigid programming languages. Oftentimes, programs require students to display logic, insight, and abstract thinking in order to successfully perform within the program. This is a function of the rigid requirements of computer programming, not individual programs. Whereas the human brain is very flexible and can recognize partially correct responses or correct portions of wrong answers, computers can recognize as correct only items that have been programmed as correct.

It is possible for authors to accommodate the special needs of young users when writing their programs. For example, *any* key in a section of the keyboard may be accepted as a correct response, instead of only one specific key. Evaluators need to consider the elements within a specific program and then decide whether there is an appropriate match between the software and its requirements and the potential users and their abilities. If there is a good match, the program will help users with the learning task instead of interfering with overly specific or distracting requirements for interaction.

There are prerequisite skills for any software program. In the evaluation of software, prerequisite skills should first be identified. This information may be written in the documentation or implied through the content of the program. The program itself should build upon these already developed or learned, prerequisite skills. Young students cannot learn the concept of alphabetical order until they can recite the alphabet, nor are algebraic concepts taught until the student has some background in basic arithmetic. Once the prerequisite skills have been identified, the evaluator must determine whether they match the target audience (i.e., the students who will be using the program). Second graders usually can recite the alphabet, but they are not yet ready for high school algebra lessons. Both content built on the prerequisite skills, and an appropriate match between those skills and the target audience are necessary for a good program.

Similarly, the reading level of program instructions should match the content level of material presented. An arithmetic program on missing addends is probably designed for first or second graders. If the directions on the disk are written on the fifth or sixth grade level, students may have trouble using the software. Also, programs for high school students should not have instructions written for early elementary children. When designed for a nonreading audience, some programs now give oral directions.

Producers of educational software should consider the developmental level of users in other ways, too. The type of response required by the program should be based on characteristics of the user. It would probably be unreasonable to expect preschool children to pick out specific letters on the keyboard to answer the program. One producer handles this by dividing the keyboard into general areas and telling adults how to use a ribbon to mark the areas for children. On the other hand, it is probably reasonable to assume that high school students can either type or pick out the correct key(s) for more complicated responses.

Some producers show consideration for the age of their anticipated audience in the way the computer screen is designed. Programs for young users should be more open and uncluttered than those for older students. Also, it is possible for the lettering to be larger for primary students, in the same way that controlled vocabulary books are printed in larger type. For beginning readers, the shape of the alphabetic characters and numerals becomes very important. While adults and older children can be flexible enough to recognize letters in different typefaces or styles, young children can be easily confused by computer-generated scripts. It is possible to use the computer's graphic capabilities to present more conventional letters in programs where this may be a problem.

Finally, there should be nothing in the software which would alienate the student users. For example, a particular reading program may be well suited to work with a remedial eighth grade class, but if the title indicates it is for use with the ''average fourth grade student,'' this labeling will probably interfere with whatever benefit the junior high students may derive from the software. Other software may be condescending or even rude in remarks directed at users. It is usually better to avoid such software.

Environmental Considerations

In addition to the inherent characteristics discussed above, evaluators of educational software must consider the school environment in which it will be used. Before purchasing a program, the teacher or school library media specialist should know how, when, where, and how often students will probably work with it. Some programs are too repetitious for certain students, and don't repeat enough for others. It makes better sense to purchase expensive programs only if there is a reasonable expectation of frequent usage. Complicated programs may be inappropriate if students will work them for only ten or fifteen minutes at a time. If students need to spend a considerable amount of time learning the rules for a particular program, its use may be limited to situations where the users can have large blocks of time to work with it.

When several students are expected to work together with a particular program, the software should have been designed to allow this interaction. Large, clear screen presentation and time for group interaction between required responses can help make it easier for multiple users.

Summary

Indications of Educational Quality

A. Production Concerns
1. Authors have background or training in education
2. Program was pretested and revised
3. Possible to identify program goal(s) and objectives
4. Enhances, supports, and supplements school objectives
B. Presentation of Information
1. Material organized in small, well-sequenced units
2. Information or skill presented more than once
3. Builds from the familiar to the new or unknown
4. Required user response matches the program objectives
C. Suitable for Intended Audience
1. Program requirements match the developmental and/or intellectual level of target audience

2. Prerequisite skills match both the program and the target audience
3. Reading level of program and program instructions appropriate for the target audience
4. Type of response required consistent with the skills of target audience
5. Computer screen adapted for young users, where appropriate
6. Neither content nor documentation is offensive to students
7. Type and amount of anticipated use is compatible with the program

SELECTED SOURCES

Cohen, Vicki Blum. "Criteria for the Evaluation of Microcomputer Courseware," *Educational Technology* 23 (January 1983): 9–14.

Keogh, James Edward. "The Classroom Crystal Ball," *Microcomputing* 6 (February 1982): 94–98.

Kingman, James C. "Designing Good Educational Software," *Creative Computing* 7 (October 1981): 72–81.

Kleiman, Glenn; Mary M. Humphrey; and Trudy Van Buskirk. "Evaluating Educational Software," *Creative Computing* 7 (October 1981): 84–90.

Raleigh, C. Patrick. "Give Your Child a Head Start," *Personal Software* 1 (November 1983): 36–53.

Test, David W. "Evaluating Educational Software for the Microcomputer," *Journal of Special Education Technology* 7 (Summer 1985): 37–46.

4

Documentation and Support Materials

When microcomputer software programs are purchased, instructions on how to use them should be included, either in the program itself or in the more traditional printed format. These operating instructions are frequently called *documentation*. Sometimes student worksheets, suggested activities, or other support materials are also included. This chapter will consider those items which accompany the educational software programs.

Printed Documentation

Usually a program will be sold with directions for its use in a printed paper-and-ink format. This documentation can be a printed sheet or sheets, a pamphlet, a loose leaf manual, or a bound book. Generally, simple and noncomplex programs have little documentation, and complex programs are accompanied by instruction books or loose leaf manuals.

In the past, most documentation was poorly written and often confusing. Producers and programmers were accused of writing instructions that were intelligible only to other computer programmers and, therefore, indecipherable by the general public. Fortunately, this situation is changing for the better.

Good documentation should include clear and complete directions on the operation of its program. The user should be able to sit at the computer, follow the directions in the documentation, and successfully operate the program. Poor instructions can cause confusion and frustration, especially when important information is missing and the program doesn't perform as anticipated. A trial-and-error search for the correct key to advance the screen, for example, should not be necessary.

Furthermore, the documentation should be well constructed. The information should be presented in a logical order—from how to begin the program, to using it, through finishing the exercise. Otherwise, the user could be paging back and forth while searching for the instructions needed to continue the program. Also, it is helpful if information for the basic operation of the program is presented first and the more complex or advanced operations are left for later discussion.

In some cases, illustrations, especially reproductions of selected screens within the program itself, make it easier for the reader to follow the instructions. For more complex programs with more detail, an index, section headings, or table of contents can be invaluable, provided they are well designed. A poor index, for example, may not list terms under their most common usage, but hide them (so to speak) under broader or narrower categories. It may also be necessary to teach students how to use an index or table of contents effectively. Ideally, these aids could allow the experienced user to locate needed information on demand.

The quality of the printing is also important. Earlier documentation was occasionally presented on poor-quality mimeograph sheets. More recent efforts are usually of acceptable quality, and some are very well done.

In addition to instructions on use of the program, the documentation could, and probably should, indicate how teachers and school library media specialists can help students get the most educational benefit from the program. A discussion of pretesting and the resultant changes in the program should be given in the documentation as another indication of the software's quality and possible application. This is also the place to discuss program features, advantages, and limitations. For example, if the software uses a branching technique to react in various ways to different user responses, the documentation could detail the different branches or paths used by the program. It is possible for a teacher or media specialist to determine—eventually—how a program reacts by giving a variety of responses, but this tends to be time consuming. Similarly, if the producer has elected to limit—say—a Spanish-language program to regular verbs, the documentation should explain why this decision was made, instead of leaving the evaluator to guess at a justification. In the *Snooper Troops* program, the user must gather clues from the town depicted on the computer monitor as a map. The documentation does not include a copy of the town's map, because the producers believe users can enhance their mapping skills by drawing their own as they work with the software. When this type of information is included in the documentation, it can help the teacher or media specialist make a more informed decision about program purchase or use. The programmer or producer know their own product well enough to provide this type of information more easily than the teacher or librarian can discover it independently.

Printed documentation is also the place to discuss those sections of the program that should be protected and not open to ready student access. For example, some software has a section which records student scores and/or evaluates student performance. Directions on how to access this part of the program, use it, and change the password (which gives access to student scores) should be protected in order to guard privileged information and students' privacy. Nevertheless, the documentation should give clear, uncomplicated guidance to the understanding and use of the information management section so teachers and media specialists can take full advantage of this time-saving device. At the same time, students should not be allowed access to such confidential information about this section in printed documentation. Instead, two sets of instructions may be provided, one for teachers and media specialists and one for students. An alternative way to protect this section is to provide printed documentation only for education professionals, and give directions for using the program on the disk.

Documentation in the Program

With increasing frequency, some or most of the operating instructions for microcomputer software are in the program itself. Ideally, the user should be able to insert the program into the microcomputer and run it by following *only* those directions which appear on the screen or monitor. An introductory section, or *tutorial,* could explain the functions of certain keys which will be used in the operation of the program.

As with printed instructions, documentation which is part of the software should be clear, concise, and easy to follow. Most programs give rudimentary instructions on the screen while the program is operating. Such comments as "Use spacebar for next screen" or "Now push return" can remind students of the appropriate response and thereby decrease frustration. Students should be able to operate the software independently, which frees the teacher to pursue other classroom activities.

Some programs have a "window" on the screen that lists the most commonly used operations of the program. *Bank Street Writer,* a word processing program, employs this technique to list popular commands that are used to input and edit material. If this approach is not used, a method should be devised to allow users to ask for help when they need it.

Other programs direct new users through a series of screens designed to teach them how to use the program. This type of section could show which keys are used to move the cursor in different directions, how to change or shift objects shown on the screen, and similar instructions. While necessary for beginning users, experienced students do not need this type of information every time they use the program. Therefore, an alternative approach should allow experienced users to bypass the beginners' instructions and proceed directly to the program.

One strategy that teachers and librarians can follow is to run the program first and then return to the more complete documentation, either in printed format or within the program, for the finer points, special functions, and procedures which may have been missed.

Support Materials

In addition to operating instructions and information, some educational software programs are accompanied by items which can be used to reinforce or extend topics presented within the program. Some producers include these materials because it is not usually possible for an entire class to use a program at the same time. When supplemental worksheets and/or suggested activities complement and extend the program, they can be effective and worthwhile. Since they are included with some programs, evaluators need to judge their quality before using them with students. On the other hand, poor supplemental materials alone are usually not a sufficient reason for rejecting the entire program.

Worksheets which are correlated with the program can help students continue work on relevant skills when they are away from the computer. Potentially valuable, these worksheets should be evaluated in the same fashion as other educational seat work which is not associated with microcomputer software. They should be well designed so students can read and write on them easily. They should present educationally sound information which is truly supplementary and which does not merely duplicate items within the computer program. The teacher or media specialist should be given permission to copy the worksheets as necessary, or duplication masters should be included in the documentation.

Occasionally, follow-up activities or areas for further exploration are suggested. Again, as with worksheets, the teacher or media specialist needs professional expertise to judge the appropriateness of such activities.

As a rule, a software program and accompanying materials should be self-contained. That is, if the student is referred from the computer program to another item, such as the detective's case book in *Snooper Troops,* that item should be included in the purchased materials. Occasionally, it could be appropriate for the program to refer to an item the classroom or library could be expected to have, for example, a dictionary. But such occurrences should be kept to a minimum.

Summary

A. Printed Documentation
1. Includes clear, complete directions on operation of the program
2. Is presented in logical order
3. Uses good organizational aids
4. Discusses program features, advantages, and limitations
5. Contains instructions on access to and use of protected areas of the software
6. Denies students access to confidential information
B. Documentation in the Program
1. Possible to use the program only by following directions which appear on computer screen
2. Clear, concise, and easy to follow
3. Experienced users can bypass lengthy beginners' instructions
C. Support Materials
1. Educationally sound and truly supplementary, not mere duplication of the program content
2. Follow-up activities are appropriate
3. Program and accompanying materials are self-contained

SELECTED SOURCES

Cohen, Vicki Blum. "What Is Instructionally Effective Microcomputer Software?" *Viewpoints in Teaching and Learning* 59 (Spring 1983): 13–27

Collopy, David. "Software Documentation: Reading a Package by Its Cover," *Personal Computing* 7 (February 1983): 134–44.

Kingman, James C. "Designing Good Educational Software," *Creative Computing* 7 (October 1981): 72–81.

Olds, Henry F. "Evaluating Written Guides to Software," *Classroom Computer News* 2 (November/December 1982): 54.

Riordon, Tim. "How to Select Software You Can Trust," *Classroom Computer News* 3 (March 1983): 56–61.

5

User Interaction with Program

As the student works with a software program, he or she may answer questions, fill in blanks, select one of several items presented, provide information, and respond to the program in numerous ways. In turn, the program reacts to user input. The program should be written so that the student derives maximum benefit from the interaction between user and software. As much as possible, the student should be in charge.

In general, students will be working with educational software on an individual basis. That is, one student at a time will operate the program, either in the classroom or in the media center. Consequently, the program should be flexible enough to interact in different ways.

Operating Interaction

Some of the student's actions are intended to operate the software program itself; that is, they are more directional than intellectual. The student should have control over the pacing of the program, except in certain testing or typing programs. In any group of people, no two individuals will read or think at exactly the same pace. If the program automatically advanced to the next screen or to new information at a predetermined rate, some users will finish early and wait. Other users will be unable to finish one screen before the next is presented and, consequently, will miss a portion of the information. Also, the program's predetermined pace will probably be suitable for only a minority of the users who read at the same rate of speed at which the computer is presenting information.

Ideally, the student should control the pace of the program, perhaps by using the return key when he or she has finished reading a screen and is ready for the next. An alternative is to have the program allow the student to indicate one of several typing speeds for information presentation. This allows for at least some student control and individualization.

Besides controlling the pace of the software, the user sometimes needs to direct movement within the program. One student may wish to review material presented earlier, and should be able to return to earlier screens of information for this purpose. Another student may wish to stop working, and should be able to exit from the software. If extensive directions on how to run the program are on the disk, it should be possible for experienced users to skip over repetitive instructions.

There are times, of course, when users need to be able to move to specific locations within the program. Some software has a table of contents, called a *menu,* which can help users identify which portion of the program they want. A menu makes it possible for the user to go directly to the section requested.

There are certain situations, however, when the student should not be able to avoid a specified section of the program. For example, if a test is incorporated into the software to evaluate user performance, the student should not be able to skip that section. Similarly, if the teacher or media specialist has indicated the program should operate at level 3 with a certain student, that student should not be able to select level 2 or level 4. Also, some programs determine which information or question to present next from user response to the printed material. When this is well done, students should not be able to circumvent legitimate branching in order to skip needed review or avoid working with new material. Although there are exceptions, like the above, students should be able to direct movement within educational software as much as possible.

Programs should also be designed so that the student has the opportunity for interaction. Inferior programs waste time by presenting elaborate graphics, filling the screen with information, asking the student for one brief response, and then repeating the process. Thus the student can become bored or frustrated while sitting and waiting for the screen to fill. Instead, the program should be designed so that students are frequently and actively involved, both intellectually and physically.

There are many ways for the student to interact with microcomputer software, and these responses differ from program to program. The return key may be used to present the next screen in a program, while another program uses the space bar for this function. Generally, this lack of standardized response does not present a problem. Occasionally, however, microcomputer software programs use different responses for the same function in the same program. For example, the return key might advance the program in one place, but the student would be expected to use the space bar to do this same thing later in the program. This can cause students to be confused and/or frustrated. The function assigned to any particular key needs to be consistent within the program.

Furthermore, the type of student response required should be consistent with the type of learning desired, whether it is recognition, recollection, or application. To reinforce recognition, for example, the user may need to pick the correct chemical symbol from a list of five. If the program is designed to test recollection, the student should be required to give the correct answer, such as typing in or spelling the required word or words.

Programs that present situations to users in which they apply knowledge gained earlier should be a situation or question which is truly different from, although an extension of, material already presented. Sometimes there is one specific answer, as when a physics program presents a practical application of electronic theory. Sometimes the users know they are doing well when they win the game or ''survive'' the simulated dangerous journey. Sometimes there is no set answer, and the program presents a set of possibly correct responses for comparison so the students can evaluate their own thinking. The key element here is whether or not the question or situation really gives the student the opportunity to apply knowledge already gained. Whatever type of learning the program wishes to promote, the required student response should match and reinforce it.

Microcomputer software also needs to allow students to correct their own mistakes. Sometimes when students are responding to the program, they are able to identify a mistake they have made. In this case, the program should allow them to correct the error. For example, the student could backspace and retype the correct response. Most programs allow the student to correct errors, but it is impossible to do this in others. When the student is unable to correct his or her errors, the program is not helping the student learn. This can and does cause frustration.

A few software programs contain errors that interfere with their operation. For example, following instructions *correctly* may cause a program to ''crash'' or shut down. Although this type of programming mistake is rare, software that does this should not be purchased. Teachers and students have a right to expect error free, functional software.

Correct Responses

In addition to operational responses, most instructional software will ask students to indicate how well they know or have learned the material presented. Inevitably, some student responses will be correct, and then the program can react in a number of ways. Unless it is a testing situation, the student should be notified of correct answers, and the program should continue as usual. Often simple remarks, such as "That's correct" or "Great!" are sufficient. Some programs add musical fanfare to acknowledge correct answers, which students seem to enjoy. Others use animated graphics to reward correct answers. All of these responses can be appropriate, although other factors need to be taken into consideration.

Young children respond better to immediate feedback with visual or audio components. Older children, who can read more readily, can handle printed remarks like "That's correct" and will work for a delayed reward. One language arts program consists of approximately twenty minutes of reading and vocabulary exercises, followed by a timed word game which functions as a reward for students who work through the program. This technique can work well with fifth or sixth graders, but is less successful with first graders.

Variety in a program's responses to correct answers can also be desirable. For example, the same animated sequence can become overly familiar. But there is some evidence that if the "little man" jumps or waves a flag or turns somersaults in a random order, students are more interested in his activities.

Sometimes, simple acknowledgment of correct responses is sufficient. In other situations, especially if students are guessing, they may need an explanation of why the correct response is correct. Based on program content, the teacher or school library media specialist should judge whether or not such explanations are desirable when they evaluate a program.

Content Errors

Some student responses to knowledge questions will of course be incorrect, because students don't know the right answer. One purpose—perhaps the primary function—of educational software is to *help teach* the student. This means that programs should attempt to help the student who responds incorrectly.

In some cases, giving the student a second chance to respond correctly can prompt deeper thinking and compensate for a too-hasty student response. Other programs show the user which part of an answer is wrong and then wait for a second response. For example, in the software program *Gertrude's Secrets,* students are expected to select individual pieces from several pieces (which differ in color and shape) which belong in a specific box. When a student makes a mistake and releases a shape in the wrong box, it won't stay there, and falls to the bottom of the screen. The student continues to place shapes in boxes until the pattern is completed, and may even reuse those pieces which fell out. The program's non-threatening response to wrong answers (the pieces just fall out of incorrect boxes) encourages the student to continue the search for Gertrude's secret rule, and also teaches the rudiments of logic. In cases like this, giving the student a second chance can be an appropriate technique for responding to incorrect answers.

If the student persists in giving a wrong answer after the second chance, a program may repeat part of the content designed to reteach the information needed for a correct response—similar to the way a classroom teacher would repeat material in a lesson several times. Sometimes the students themselves are able to ask for a review of pertinent material or of something he or she has not understood, instead of relying on the microcomputer software to do this. Either way, by repeating the pertinent portions of the lesson, the microcomputer software supports classroom or library activities instead of serving as a "guessing game" where students keep punching keys until they discover the correct response by the process of elimination.

Another appropriate technique for handling incorrect responses is to compare the student's wrong answer to the correct one. Then the student can identify his or her mistake. This works best in simulations or problem-solving programs with more mature students who are self-motivated enough to use this information to increase their knowledge.

Ideally, educational software should attempt to diagnose student errors. At this time, however, this function is beyond the microcomputer's capabilities. Until more research in artificial intelligence has been done and practical applications of that research are possible, educational software can only identify wrong answers, not determine why the student made the error.

A "second chance," reteaching pertinent materials, and comparison between right and wrong answers are appropriate responses to wrong answers because they can support and enhance the teaching process. Unfortunately, not all software programs respond well to student errors. Some programs merely indicate that the answer is wrong and continue to the next problem. This approach does not help students understand what they did wrong and does not help them answer correctly in the future.

Some programs display an insulting message, like "That's wrong, dummy," when a student answers incorrectly. Educators should not use such derogatory language with students, and there is no excuse for a microcomputer program to do it, either. Equally troublesome are programs with an audible response to wrong answers which cannot be turned off. They proclaim to everyone within hearing distance when the user makes a mistake. Microcomputer software programs should use the same care to protect the dignity of students as classroom teachers and school library media specialists use in classroom teaching.

A flashy or elaborate response to wrong answers can also be inappropriate. When the fuse on the bomb gets shorter with each incorrect answer, it can be more entertaining to continue to give wrong answers and watch the explosion than to answer correctly. Software should be designed to encourage right answers instead of rewarding wrong ones.

Format Errors

In addition to answering incorrectly, either inadvertently or deliberately, students sometimes make mistakes in the way they type or key in their responses.

Typing errors and misspellings belong in this category of mistakes. Microcomputers tend to be totally inflexible, and most programs do not attempt to deal with typing errors or misspellings. Instead, such mistakes are treated like any other wrong answer. This can be confusing and/or frustrating for students who know the right answer but were not aware of any spelling or typing mistake, and thought they had responded correctly.

It is possible for programmers to write software which can handle these mistakes more effectively than by using the methods discussed earlier. For example, when a student is presented with a list of possible answers and asked to type in the correct response, programs often consider a misspelled word as a wrong answer. Since the program compares the student's response to the list of possible answers, a misspelled word would not match any of the words listed. Then the student could be reminded that his or her response should come from that list, and prompted to correct the spelling or typing. It would also be possible to program the microcomputer to accept the response if most of the letters match one word, provided the words on the list are not similar. While neither of these procedure proposals is appropriate for spelling or typing programs, they could help decrease student confusion and frustration where content is of primary concern.

In addition to answering questions about the content or concepts of particular programs, students need to make certain responses to run the program. For example, the return key may be used to advance to the next screen. Frequently, nothing happens if a recognizable command is not entered, and the student has to keep trying. Another alternative is to have the program, in the case of inappropriate commands, display the alternatives for the student in order to prompt a command to which the program can then respond.

Programs can also be written to prompt students when a particular format is required for the student's response. For example, a program on graphing which requires a comma between two numbers could ask, "Are you typing a comma?" Many word processing programs, including *Bank Street Writer,* use prompts and brief statements of the functions of different keys throughout the program. Giving an example of an appropriate answer is another technique which can be used to show students how to answer questions or input responses. These devices can help reduce student frustration and increase the effectiveness of the software.

Summary

    A. Operating Interaction
      1. Student controls pace of the program
      2. Student can control direction of program, when appropriate
      3. Frequent opportunities for student interaction
      4. Function assigned to a particular key is consistent throughout program.
      5. Type of student response matches desired type of learning
      6. Students can correct their mistakes
    B. Program Response to Correct Answers
      1. Acknowledges and/or rewards correct answers
      2. Young children need immediate feedback; older ones will work for delayed reward
      3. Variety in responses to correct answers is desirable
    C. Content Errors
      1. Appropriate responses to mistakes:
        a. Give student second chance to respond
        b. Repeat part of program to reteach information needed by student for correct answer
        c. Compare student's wrong answer to correct one so he or she can identify own error
      2. Poor responses to mistakes:
        a. Identify answer as wrong and continue to next problem or section
        b. Display insulting or derogatory message
        c. Audible response to wrong answers
        d. Flashy, elaborate response to wrong answers

D. Format Errors (e.g., Typing or Spelling Errors)
   1. Should not be handled in same manner as content errors
   2. Some options are available:
      a. Prompt the student if answer does not match one of predetermined selections
      b. Accept minor misspellings if most of the letters match
   3. When incorrect command is used, program should
      a. Wait for appropriate command
      b. Prompt student by displaying available choices of correct commands

SELECTED SOURCES

Cohen, Vicki Blum. "Criteria for the Evaluation of Microcomputer Courseware," *Educational Technology* 23 (January 1983): 9–14.

Gallagher, Francine L. "What Educators Want in Microcomputer Software," *Catholic Library World* 55 (February 1984): 290–93.

Kleiman, Glenn; Mary M. Humphrey; and Trudy Van Buskirk. "Evaluating Educational Software," *Creative Computing* 7 (October 1981): 84–90.

Raleigh, C. Patrick. "Give Your Child a Head Start," *Personal Software* 1 (November 1983): 36–53.

Riordon, Tim. "How to Select Software You Can Trust," *Classroom Computer News* 3 (March 1983): 56–61.

Test, David W. "Evaluating Educational Software for the Microcomputer," *Journal of Special Education Technology* 7 (Summer 1985): 37–46.

6

Utilization of Microcomputer Strengths

Because microcomputers are capable of handling large amounts of data quickly and efficiently, educational software should exploit this strength to provide flexible and creative learning experiences for students. This chapter will discuss specific ways programs can use the microcomputer's ability to react to and control numerous pieces of information.

Programming Uses of Computer Strengths

Microcomputer software programs should be branching-type programs, not linear ones. In a linear program, every user answers every question in the same sequence: question 1, question 2, question 3, and so on. The program does not accommodate different learning skills and speeds. In a branching program, the next question or sequence is determined by user response to the present inquiry. One student may go from question 1 to question 2, while another student goes from question 1 to question 10. If a student responds incorrectly to a question about the program's concepts, the material can be reviewed or presented again and again, until he or she demonstrates mastery. A student who responds correctly can progress to new material and avoid unnecessary review.

The purpose of a branching program is to accommodate different answers—to be able to give needed repetition in instruction to some students while advancing those who are ready. It is also possible for such a program to present material or problems with gradual increases in complexity or difficulty. For example, arithmetic problems may start with two addends and move to five or six, or a Spanish-language program may go from regular to irregular verbs. A branching program helps to individualize classroom instruction by tailoring the learning experience to each student.

31

Any software program should be more than a workbook transferred to the computer. Examination of the program should show something over and above the traditional workbook material, for example, branching, or the ability to provide additional problems for students who need more work. A workbook might be equally effective and considerably cheaper, but computer capability gives the advantage.

One advantage to the microcomputer is immediate feedback. Students will know, in most cases, whether their answers are right or wrong before new material is presented. This is a distinct advantage over paper-and-pencil work, which is corrected by the instructor and returned at a later time.

If the program presents a series of problems—arithmetic exercises, vocabulary matching, etc.—these exercises should be presented in random order. That is, the specific problems presented to the student should not be given in the same sequence every time. This variety helps to ensure that students are responding to the content of the program, instead of memorizing the correct answers in order of appearance.

If there is a timed segment in the program, the software itself should keep track of elapsed time. If students have three minutes to find as many small words as they can within one large word, the program itself should time the activity, and notify players when it is time to quit. This can be done by having the program refuse further input. Students would be distracted if they have to watch the classroom clock, too.

The Screen

The program should be designed to make maximum use of the computer monitor screen. Information on the screen should never be crowded or cluttered. Printing should be clear and easy to read. For this reason, double-spacing is recommended for all text, and large type may enhance a program for young students. Controlled vocabulary texts are printed in large type for beginning readers, and microcomputer software programs could do this as well.

Programmers could also use the graphics capability of the microcomputer to emphasize key words. Extra-bright or flashing letters could be used to attract student attention. Care must be taken, however, to avoid overusing this technique.

Graphics can be used to add interest and increase understanding. A simulation program about a nuclear reactor uses graphics to show the relationship between such components as pumps, water filters, and water flow. Graphics must be distinct, understandable, and well designed.

Color is sometimes an integral part of the program, but sometimes it is merely "window dressing." If it is an important part of the program, a color monitor is mandatory. In *Gertrude's Secrets,* some of the shapes or game pieces are identical except for color. Sometimes the shape is used to distinguish between correct and incorrect responses. Other times, color is the determining factor. In order to use this program, a color monitor is mandatory. Sometimes the documentation will indicate this requirement; sometimes this is discovered only when the software is previewed.

Sometimes color is used only for aesthetic, not educational, purposes. This is not bad if effective shading of the graphics allows the student to use some programs with a green screen or a monitor without color capabilities. For example, color graphics enhance *Snooper Troops,* but the program works perfectly well without color. If a color monitor is available, evaluators can be less concerned about this criterion. If a color monitor is *not* available, it is best not to purchase software which needs color capabilities to be used properly.

Sound

More microcomputers are equipped to produce sound now than three or four years ago. As a result, more microcomputer software programs are taking advantage of this capability, especially the ability to produce music.

Some programs are designed to help teach music. One teaches students to identify which series of musical sounds (in a set of four) are identical and which are different. Others allow students to write their own compositions and then play them back. In this type of program, sound is obviously mandatory.

Some programs for nonreaders are being designed to give oral instructions and use sound to present information. Again, in this case, sound is mandatory.

Many programs use sound to enhance the presentation or to respond to student answers. However, sound should never be used to identify a wrong response. This may encourage wrong answers if students find the noise entertaining or amusing. It also announces a student's wrong answer, which he or she may prefer not to advertise. Sound can also be used to enhance information. One program for young children is designed to teach or reinforce concepts of above and below. When an "above" answer is given, the musical response ascends the scale. Descending notes respond to a "below" answer.

If any program is to be used in the classroom or library, it should be possible to turn off the sound. Many programs allow the teacher or other user to eliminate the sound effects by hitting one key, and to restore them in the same way. If it is not possible to turn off the sound, students, teachers, and others in the vicinity could be distracted (and perhaps frustrated) by the continual audible responses, if the program is used very often.

An overall consideration should be whether or not software is the best medium for presenting the concepts in the program. If realistic motion is required, film would be the best media choice. A sound filmstrip can be best for a story-sharing situation with a large audience, and accurately portrays the artist's style. At other times, software can be best, especially when it takes full advantage of the capabilities of the microcomputer.

Summary

Ways to Exploit the Microcomputer's Data Handling Capabilities

A. In the Programming:
  1. Uses branching instead of linear programming
  2. Is more than just a computerized workbook
  3. Gives immediate feedback
  4. Problems presented in random order
B. On the Screen:
  1. Screen not crowded or cluttered
  2. Graphics emphasize or highlight key points
  3. Color an integral part of instruction
  4. Effective shading for use with noncolor monitor
C. Sound Capability
  1. Sound is used to
    a. Teach music
    b. Give oral directions
    c. Enhance presentation
    d. Reward correct answers
  2. Sound can easily be turned off

SELECTED SOURCES

Cohen, Vicki Blum. "Criteria for the Evaluation of Microcomputer Courseware," *Educational Technology* 23 (January 1983): 9–14.

Hakes, Barbara. "Selecting Microcomputer Software," *Wyoming Library Roundup* 39 (Spring/Summer 1984): 46–48.

Kleiman, Glenn; Mary M. Humphrey; and Trudy Van Buskirk. "Evaluating Educational Software," *Creative Computing* 7 (October 1981): 84–90.

7

Instructional Management

As was stated earlier, one microcomputer strength is its ability to deal with large amounts of data very efficiently. Some microcomputer software programs exploit this strength effectively by creating an instructional management segment to support the teaching function. These segments record the progress of the users and free the teacher for other classroom activities.

Student Scores

In its simplest form, the instructional management portion saves the final scores of student users for the teacher to check later. This information is stored in the program itself, and teachers and media specialists follow a specified procedure (generally a ''secret'' password) to gain access. Some older software could deal with only one student at a time, which meant the teacher had to check the program after each student finished. Some of the newer programs can store information for 120 or more students, which is much more practical for busy teachers. They can check all study scores at once, instead of continually interrupting their daily activities.

The instructional management portions of educational software are becoming more flexible and detailed. In addition to the final score, some programs will identify specific problems or types of problems the student answered incorrectly. Better programs even differentiate between correct answers on the first try and correct answers on subsequent tries.

This information can be reported in several ways, usually in table-type format. A final score for each student may be given, with no additional breakdown of student performance. It is possible to list the number of each question and whether or not the student answered it correctly. Often it is better to list portions of the test by category (e.g., reading-comprehension items) and then indicate the number of items given and the number answered correctly. Some programs categorize correct student responses into those answered on the first try, those answered on the second try, those answered on the third try, and so on. In situations where it can be helpful, some programs will monitor and record the amount of time a student takes to respond. This additional capacity makes possible a more precise evaluation of student performance by identifying specific areas of strength and weakness. Ultimately, it is the teacher's responsibility to judge when students have mastered the content of the program, but a detailed recording of student performance greatly assists this process.

Other Management Functions

Some instructional management sections do more than just record test or program scores. An initial quiz may be used to assess student entry-level skills; the results are then used to match a student's ability to the appropriate level of program difficulty. Other programs— usually the longer, multifaceted ones—use results of one portion of the entire program to prescribe which of the succeeding portions would be most appropriate. While these programmed decisions can be quite helpful, there are times when the teacher or media specialist wants or needs to specify a particular level of difficulty or a program segment for a particular student. This means that the software needs to be designed to allow the teacher to overrule these program decisions quickly and easily.

Occasionally, a program goes beyond recording student scores to diagnosing specific areas of strength or weakness. For example, a language arts program may note that a student has trouble identifying synonyms when they are used in context. While diagnostic features can be useful, they are usually not as important to the teacher as an efficient method for recording student responses to a quiz or program. When the recordkeeping system is well designed, a teacher can generally identify student strengths and weaknesses without difficulty.

It can be especially helpful if the instructional management section is capable of *printing out* the information stored in it. This means the teacher is not required to spend time at the computer to evaluate student performance. A *printout* supplies a permanent copy of students' work, and can be useful when a teacher communicates with parents.

Ease of Use

Ideally, the instructional management portion of a software program will be designed for easy use. Once into the management portion of the program, the teacher should be able to add or delete student names, look at individual student records, print out class lists or scores, and perform other similar operations. There should also be a detailed menu or directory of operations. Once the area of interest has been selected, instructions or prompts on the screen should be unambiguous and easy to follow. Since this portion of the program is designed to help teachers, it must be both functional and uncomplicated.

Security of the instructional management section is also important. It would be inappropriate for students to have ready access to their own scores and to those of their fellow students. Easy access also raises the temptation to change, erase, or add to information in this section. Most programmers set up a special procedure and a specific password, both described in the teacher's manual, to protect an instructional management section. Some programs establish a simple procedure, part of the section itself, for changing the password.

Packaging

"Packaging" refers to the box or envelope which contains the disk and any accompanying materials. While not as important as the quality of the software and documentation, evaluators should determine whether or not the packaging is adequate. In some cases it may be necessary to transfer the purchased materials to other containers. This may be done for uniformity and easier storage, or because the quality of the packaging is too poor. In any case, poor packaging is not usually a sufficient reason for not purchasing a program.

Summary

Instructional Management Section
A. Records Student Scores
   1. Saves final scores for a number of students
   2. Identifies specific types of problems which give students difficulty
   3. Differentiates between correct answers on first tries and correct answers on subsequent tries

B. Other Management Functions
1. Uses student performance to determine portion of program to be presented
2. Gives initial diagnosis of student's ability
3. Capable of printing out its information
C. Must Be Easy to Use
D. Security Procedures Protect Its Information

SELECTED SOURCES

Anderson, Eric. "Software Selection Considerations," *ACCESS: Microcomputers in Libraries* 2 (July 1982): 10–11.

Bland, Barbara B. "Evaluation: The Key to Selecting Quality Microcomputer Courseware for School Media Collections," *North Carolina Libraries* 40 (Fall/Winter 1982): 191–97 + .

Cohen, Vicki Blum. "Criteria for the Evaluation of Microcomputer Courseware," *Educational Technology* 23 (January 1983): 9–14.

8

Characteristics of Formats

The previous chapters have discussed some specific criteria which can be used to evaluate educational microcomputer software. While these criteria can be applied to all types of programs, there are special considerations which apply only to specific formats. In this chapter, items will be presented which can guide the examination of drill and practice programs, tutorials, simulations, games, problem solving, and shell programs.

Drill and Practice

A drill and practice program reinforces previous instruction given in the classroom or media center. The student applies or practices the knowledge or skills presented earlier until he or she masters them or reaches a predetermined level of proficiency. Drill and practice programs emphasize recognition or recollection, not application of knowledge. Their intent is not to promote original thinking, but to provide repetition needed for certain types of learning. Since the software is designed to support earlier instruction, it is vital that the skills or knowledge emphasized in the program match those taught in the classroom. These prerequisite skills may be identified in the documentation or through an examination of the software itself. But the teacher or media specialist should ensure that there is compatibility between software content and the preceding instruction.

Because they are (or should be) designed to pose as many problems as necessary, drill and practice programs *should* be repetitious. For this reason, is it usually better if the software is highly interactive. Frequent user response tends to keep the student more involved than a program which draws elaborate graphics while the student watches.

Drill and practice software should present exercises to the student in random order. That is, question 1 for student 1 should *not* be question 1 for student 2. By changing the order in which exercises are presented, software helps to keep students interested in the questions. It also becomes impossible for a student to complete the program by memorizing the answers instead of mastering the material.

Furthermore, the user should control the pace of the program, not the software itself. The next screen or question should be presented *only* after the student indicates he or she is ready for it, either by pressing a key or answering the question. Everybody reads and thinks at different speeds. What is right for one student will be either too slow or too fast for others. In general, the user should control the pace of the program. (Software designed to increase the speed of student responses, like a typing program, is the exception to this rule.)

The better drill and practice software will have progressive levels of difficulties. When the child learns to spell cat, the program moves on to house. After mastering basic arithmetic facts (2 + 2 = ?), the student practices with slightly more difficult problems (11 + 7 = ?). A secondary student may progress from regular to irregular verb conjugations in a foreign-language program. Word problems in arithmetic may be presented, if the basic procedure used to solve the problem is the same and students need practice in decoding the words.

Students master skills and knowledge at varying rates of speed, which means some students need more repetition than others. By using a branching technique, software can be more responsive to the needs of individual learners. If the answers indicate that a student has mastered one part of the program, he or she can move up to the next level of difficulty. Another user may be given additional practice on the same level, or even returned to a lower level if he or she has trouble making the transfer. Some programs even *explain* the material if too many wrong answers are given. This type of flexibility within a program can greatly enhance the individualization of education.

Because repetition is a necessary part of drill and practice software, it may be somewhat difficult to maintain student attention. Branching programs, user control of the pace, and randomization of exercises help to keep the software interesting. It is also important to reward students for correct answers, usually by a graphic or musical response. Variety in these displays and responses also helps to keep students involved. If a little man on the screen dances one time, perhaps he can turn somersaults the next. Equally important, wrong answers should not be rewarded; instead, they should be acknowledged and used to guide students to the correct answer.

A good drill and practice program can really assist classroom or media center instruction. It frees the teacher or media specialist from the need to provide the repetitious oral or written exercises required for student learning. Furthermore, the microcomputer is endlessly patient; it can drill students as long as required without becoming restless or irritated by slow learners.

Tutorial

Educational software programs which are tutorial assume some of the task of teaching. The assumption is that the student has had only minimal instruction in the skill or concept before he or she sits down at the microcomputer. The program then presents definitions, a limited concept, new Spanish words, or other information to the student; provides an opportunity for practice with or application of the material presented; and tests for mastery of the information covered. The program does not merely supplement formal teaching; in some instances it replaces it. This means that the software must be carefully checked to ensure that good educational practices are followed.

For a tutorial program to be successful, the information needs to be presented in a logical sequence. Entry-level skills must be used as the starting point and succeeding information presented in logical order, in clear and progressive steps. To teach alphabetization, the program might assume knowledge of letters and the ability to recite the alphabet. Then words with different initial letters could be used to introduce the concept, starting with widely dispersed letters and working up to those close together in the alphabet. Words with the same first letter could then be introduced, and so on.

This technique, based on a logical sequential presentation of information, is appropriate for learners of all ages and all stages of development. The size of each step, the pace of instruction, and the amount of repetition should be determined by the age and knowledge of the user.

The developmental levels of students will vary with grade and ability levels, and educational software is usually designed for a particular grade or grades. But the developmental levels also differ from individual to individual within every grade or age group. Software which uses the branching technique is better able to accommodate user differences. When branching is used, student responses determine what information will be presented next. The program may proceed to the next idea, continue work on the same level, or return to a presentation or review of earlier material. The choice is made on the basis of student responses, which ef-

41

fectively individualizes instruction *if* the program is well done. The user should be advanced to the next level or given new material *only* after mastering current-level content.

As with drill and practice programs, material should be presented with variety. This helps combat students' boredom and increases their attention span, and can thereby increase the amount of learning which occurs.

Of necessity, testing in tutorial software should be frequent. This allows for better and more accurate evaluation of student performance. Testing after each new concept or skill is imparted pinpoints problems, whereas a measure of student achievement after several concepts have been covered necessitates either further testing or risky guesswork to identify the source of confusion.

Of course, the student should be rewarded for correct answers in tutorial programs, as with software in general. Wrong answers should be used to guide later instruction, and the student should not be belittled for making mistakes.

Since tutorial programs assume part of the task of teaching students, they must be carefully evaluated to determine how well they are designed to do this job. Good tutorial programs can support and extend classroom or media center instruction.

Problem Solving

Programs which require problem solving of their users go beyond the responses to tutorial and drill and practice software. In a problem-solving situation, the student is usually asked to use previous knowledge, combine it in a new way, and "discover" a solution. The program does not teach directly; rather, it encourages the user to think and search for the answer by using information and skills the student already possesses. This should develop the user's ability to solve problems and think independently.

In this fashion, the user is taken beyond the repetition of basic exercises which are part of the drill and practice or tutorial programs. If the student does not apply the prerequisite skills or knowledge required by the program, he or she will not be able to give an appropriate or correct answer. The program does not attempt to teach prerequisite skills; instead, it sets the stage for the student to apply them.

Problem-solving software can be flexible enough to use student input to vary the situation (or situations) by allowing or encouraging the exploration of "what if" inquiries, based on user responses. In this way, students can be guided in the examination of many facets of a situation and begin to see the interrelationships of a problem.

For example, Gertrude the Goose presents students with an empty box and a set of variously colored and shaped game pieces. While trying to determine which shapes or colors belong in Gertrude's square, the student is able to ask, "What will happen if I put a blue box in the square? What if it's a red triangle?" Eventually, the user is able to identify which color or shape belongs in the box. The shape or color required changes each time the program runs. *Gertrude's Secrets* uses the problem-solving format for young children, but programs for older students are more complicated. Advanced levels of *Rocky's Boots* challenge adult users to build a Rube Goldberg device and watch it in action.

It can be helpful if the software shows the resultant reaction, good or bad, which occurs when the user makes a decision or inputs data. This explanation can be either verbal or graphic. For instance, when the user places a red triangle in Gertrude's square, it stays there if it fits the current rule for the square. If it does not belong in the box, the triangle falls to the bottom of the screen.

Problem-solving software can also help the student understand algorithmic methods. As students directly experience situations in which a rule or law guides specific decisions in a variety of instances, they can use this structural model to guide their thinking. Whereas drill and practice programs and tutorial software emphasize recollection and recognition, problem-solving programs stress application. Instead of being given an opportunity to respond with an answer or procedure to determine an answer which has been taught, a student must independently and creatively apply what he or she knows in a new way to arrive at an answer.

The microcomputer can bring a great deal to the presentation of problem-solving situations. Because the microcomputer can control and manipulate large amounts of data quickly and easily, a problem-solving program can be supported by many relevant details and respond quickly and appropriately to a wide variety of student responses. This enhances the educational value of this type of software.

Problem-solving situations may stand alone and be the only technique in a particular piece of software. More frequently, they are elements within other programs, especially games or simulations. Any time a user is asked to apply knowledge or skills he or she already possesses to discover a solution, the user is being presented with a problem-solving situation.

Games

Games can be defined as contests based on skills and/or chance that are played according to rules. Two or more students may be competing with each other, or an individual may be trying to beat the clock or the microcomputer. Only games which are used as instructional tools will be considered here, instead of those used merely to reward students. However, almost any game can have educational value when the teacher or media specialist is able to match the skills needed to play the game with the educational objectives to be emphasized. For example, Monopoly gives players practice handling money, buying and selling property, and planning strategy. Students apply both spelling and arithmetic skills while playing Scrabble.

For microcomputer games, too, the objectives of the program should support the instructional objectives. In *Snooper Troops,* as in *Clue,* players are asked to collect information to identify the guilty party from an array of suspects. Mapping skills, recordkeeping, and deductive reasoning are some of the "academic" skills that students employ in solving the mystery. An appropriate match should emphasize the instructional value of the program over that of the game format.

Since students vary in their mastery of the skills needed to play a particular game, varying levels of difficulty can increase the usefulness of the program. This can allow a student who becomes proficient at one level to advance to a more difficult level and further develop his or her skills. It can also allow slower students to work at a more comfortable level. It is appropriate that the complexity of a game increase with the level of difficulty. Instead of trying to identify shapes and colors that belong in one box, the student may be asked to work with two boxes and their intersection. Variety in the level of difficulty and complexity of a software program can greatly increase the number of students who could enjoy using it.

In an educational software game, results should depend on user input and responses, not on chance alone. The knowledge or skill needed to run the program is truly emphasized if the student must apply it to play and win the game. Otherwise, the program probably has little or no educational value.

If the game requires a great amount of playing time, it is helpful if the student can exit from the program at any point and resume play later. Especially in an educational setting, large blocks of time are not always available for a student to spend with the microcomputer. If he or she can stop and start again later, the student will probably be less frustrated, more interested, and learn more in the long run. If the user can be expected to complete the game in a reasonable amount of time (10–20 minutes), this feature is less important.

Finally, educational games should be fun to play. That is, they should be interesting and entertaining so that students will be motivated to continue to play. If students enjoy the process, more learning is likely to occur. There are very good educational software programs in the game format which students like to run.

Simulations

A simulation is designed to *represent* real-life activities by providing the essential elements of the real situation. This allows the student to apply knowledge gained in the classroom to a "real-world" situation. The presented activities are, or may be, inappropriate for students to experience directly because of cost, hazards, or time constraints. With the microcomputer's ability to store and manipulate large amounts of data, software can be written which presents very detailed and often realistic simulations. By giving the student the feeling of "you are there," simulation can stimulate interest and encourage learning in many diverse areas, such as history (re-create a Civil War battle), engineering ("What if I use these specifications for building the bridge?"), or chemistry ("If these two substances are combined, will they explode?"). One such program challenges the user to operate the Three Mile Island nuclear reactor while avoiding meltdown and showing an overall profit for the electric company. Designed for older students, the program can challenge the user while increasing his or her understanding of nuclear reactors.

As with games, the objectives of the simulation should match and support the instructional objectives of the teacher or media specialist. There should be varying and progressive levels of difficulty, and user responses should determine the results of the program. For complex and/or time-consuming software, users should be able to stop their participation, and resume it later, without redoing the program from the beginning. Finally, the software should maintain students' interest.

Some considerations apply *only* to simulations. When writing a simulation, the programmer must analyze the situation, problem, or process to identify the essential elements which *must* be included in the software. Within the program, furthermore, the programmer must identify and present the interrelationships among the program's elements in a way that represents reality while omitting unnecessary portions. Although the reactor and containment buildings and their contents are necessary portions of the Three Mile Island program, the physical dimensions of these structures can be omitted.

A simulation needs to depict a real-life situation with realistic outcomes based on student input. The program should be exciting enough to maintain student interest but, at the same time, avoid events which are too bizarre and unrealistic. Pioneers on the Oregon Trail may have experienced severe hailstorms, but not more than once a week.

There are times and situations when the teacher or school library media specialist needs to stipulate which options the program will impose on a simulation. This type of control can be used to tailor the software to classroom activities. In this way, the simulation can give users a chance to apply newly gained insights or explore questions raised in class discussion.

The sophistication level of the simulation should be appropriate for the students who will be using it. A simulation of Three Mile Island is probably best suited to high school students, but a program based on the western movement along the Oregon Trail could be suitable for upper elementary grades.

When properly designed, a simulation can motivate and stimulate learning by promoting student involvement and thinking. All essential elements of the real situation and the interrelationships among them must be included, and student input must determine the final outcome. When these two criteria are met, simulations can be very valuable tools for promoting learning.

Shell Programs

There are programs available, called *shell programs* or *shells,* whose basic format is given on the disk, but the teacher or media specialist is able to add specific material on a topic or variety of topics. The basic design of the program remains constant, but the teacher or media specialist is allowed to design those questions which would be *most* appropriate for his or her students. While this initially places more responsibility on the educators, it can result in programs that more closely meet the needs of particular students.

This type of software often uses the drill and practice or game format. For example, the gameshow format of *Password* could be on the disk, with an emcee who delivers clues or questions to two competing teams, whose correct answers earn points. The teacher or media specialist can write and enter material on topics ranging from nursery rhymes to physics that students must respond to in order to play. Ideally, this type of software will accept both alphabetical and numerical input from teachers and school library media specialists.

It is important that these programs be easy for educators to use. Simple and clear instructions to guide the teacher or media specialist through the procedure for changing program content should be mandatory. Otherwise, shell programs may receive little use.

Some shell programs require microcomputers with two disk drives, one for the program and one for the questions and clues. This means that schools without two disk drives on their microcomputers would not be able to use such programs. On the other hand, it also means that teachers and media specialists can build a collection of second disks with questions and clues, instead of entering the material each time a unit topic changes.

The flexibility of shell programs can allow instructors to vary the level and difficulty of material for student use, which could also increase the overall utility of the programs. Aside from content, the format of the shell program may not be suitable for all students in all grades. The *Password* format is probably too advanced for nonreaders, and high school students may find participation in this "game" beneath their dignity.

Summary

A. Drill and Practice Programs
   1. Content compatible with earlier classroom instruction
   2. Repetitious
   3. Interactive
   4. Exercises presented in random order
   5. User controls pace of program
   6. Progressive levels of difficulty
   7. Use branching techniques of programming
   8. Reward correct answers; good technique for handling wrong answers
B. Tutorial Programs
   1. Assume some of the task of instruction
   2. Information presented in logical sequence
   3. Use branching techniques of programming
   4. Exercises presented in random order
   5. Frequent assessment of student performance
   6. Reward correct answers; good technique for handling wrong answers
C. Problem-solving Programs
   1. Student uses previously acquired knowledge to "discover" solution
   2. Student input influences the presented situation
   3. Reaction shown for each user action
   4. Promote understanding of algorithmic methods
   5. Contain relevant details
   6. Respond to wide variety of student responses

D. Games
   1. Objectives match instructional objectives
   2. Varying levels of difficulty available
   3. Results depend on user input, not on chance alone
   4. User can stop and resume play later, without penalty
   5. Fun to play
E. Simulations
   1. Objectives match instructional objectives
   2. Varying and progressive levels of difficulty available
   3. User responses determine results of program
   4. User can stop and resume play later, without penalty
   5. Programs are interesting
   6. Include all essential elements of real situation
   7. Interrelationships among elements are accurate
   8. Sophistication level of program matches sophistication level of anticipated users
F. Shell Programs
   1. Simple, uncomplicated procedure for changing content
   2. Accept letters *and* numbers
   3. May require two disk drives
   4. Format is appropriate for intended audience

SELECTED SOURCES

Bland, Barbara B. "Evaluation: The Key to Selecting Quality Microcomputer Courseware for School Media Collections," *North Carolina Libraries* 40 (Fall/Winter 1982): 191–97 + .

Brown, James W.; Richard B. Lewis; and Fred F. Harcleroad. *AV Instruction: Technology, Media, and Methods* (6th ed.). New York: McGraw-Hill, 1983.

Daetz, Denney. "Bellwether Social Studies Programs," *Classroom Computer Learning* 6 (November/December 1985): 46–47 + .

Dyer, Susan R., and Richard C. Forcier. "How to Pick Computer Software," *Instructional Innovator* 27 (September 1982): 38–40.

Eldredge, Bruce, and Kenneth Delp. "How to Evaluate Educational Computer Programs," *Media & Methods* 17 (March 1981): 4 + .

Kingman, James C. "Designing Good Educational Software," *Creative Computing* 7 (October 1981): 72–81.

Roberts, Nancy. "Testing the World with Simulations: When the Computer Is the Laboratory, the Subject Can Be Almost Anything," *Classroom Computer News* 3 (January/February 1983): 28–31.

9

Evaluation Procedures

In order to apply the evaluation concerns discussed in preceding chapters, the teacher or media specialist needs to identify, locate, and use specific educational software programs. This chapter will suggest some strategies for doing this.

Identifying Programs

The first step is to be aware of particular needs in a school or classroom that could be met by using a microcomputer in the instructional process. Then the problem is to identify promising software programs whose titles or descriptions indicate they may meet those needs.

There are several ways to locate potentially useful programs. Increasing numbers of journals in library and information science, education, and computer science publish reviews of educational software. While mainly descriptive, reviews generally do a good job of detailing the content of programs. These journals also publish articles about specific programs, which give a more detailed analysis of their content. These articles can be a source of additional titles.

Publishers' catalogs can also be a useful source of titles. These catalogs are designed to sell their product, and therefore have a distinct bias, but they usually give the title and a brief content description of the educational programs the producer has available for sale.

Professional conventions and meetings are another good opportunity for identifying promising titles. Some dealers or distributors of educational software display their products and are often willing to discuss these items. Sometimes a microcomputer is available, and it is possible to run a program and determine whether or not its potential usefulness warrants a more detailed analysis.

Evaluation Procedures

Oftentimes a teacher or media specialist will hear of software from his or her colleagues, which is one reason why professional organizations and national, state, regional, and local meetings are important. This informal network can quickly spread the word about good and bad software.

Obtaining Preview Copies

Once a potentially useful program has been identified, the teacher or librarian should examine it closely to determine whether or not it actually meets the needs identified in the school. It is *not* recommended that any educational software program be purchased without preview.

Software producers and distributors may be reluctant to send a program to a school on approval because it is relatively easy for a knowledgeable person to copy a program, and producers seem to be concerned about this. The teacher or media specialist can write to the dealer concerned, on letterhead stationery, asking to preview a particular program or programs and state that it is school policy never to buy software without seeing it first. Some companies require that such preview requests be sent on an approved purchase order. The letter or purchase order should guarantee that no copy of the program will be made, and it is the responsibility of the teacher or media specialist to enforce this.

If it is not possible to obtain a preview copy of a program from a dealer, other strategies may work. Throughout the country, more and more centers are being established where software is available for professionals to examine. These centers can be state or university sponsored, and some are affiliated with a school district or districts. Usually, one of the functions of such centers is to provide access to a variety of programs for educational professionals.

Exhibits at conventions offer another way to examine materials before purchase. It may be difficult, in the hectic environment of a professional meeting, to investigate a program as thoroughly as desirable, but it is better than purchasing the program without preview.

Some dealers' and distributors' sales representatives travel from school to school. Sometimes, upon request, the salesmen will leave a copy of a program with the teacher or librarian. Sometimes they will allow you to examine the program while they wait. In any case, salesmen can at times arrange for previews of their materials. Users' clubs are another source of information about software, and may have programs available for use at their site.

Examining the Program

After a title has been identified and a copy of it is available, it is time to analyze the program and evaluate its quality and potential usefulness. The examiners should be teachers or media specialists who are familiar with the need or needs the program should fulfill, the students who will use it, the content area it should cover, and who are capable of evaluating educational software. It may be necessary to have a team of professionals examine the program in order to make a fully informed judgment.

A good initial approach is to put the disk in the microcomputer and run the program. Since it is probably helpful to select software that students can handle independently, the evaluator should determine whether it is possible to use the program by following only those instructions given on the screen. This is a first look at the content and operation of the software. In addition to becoming familiar with the program in general, this first contact enables the evaluator to identify obvious flaws. For example, a program may "crash" (stop entirely or exhibit only a blank, nonresponsive screen) when directions are followed. This is a flaw in programming, and can be sufficient reason to decide against purchase.

After the evaluator is comfortable with the basic operation of the program, he or she should begin to experiment with and test the program. Creative responses can be used to gauge how the program will react to advanced students. By giving slow or incorrect answers, it is possible to analyze how the software will respond to wrong answers or slow students. Restarting the program allows the evaluator to check for branching and a random order of questions, where appropriate. Incorrect spelling and typing errors can test the flexibility of the programmer. By role-playing as advanced, regular, and slow students, an evaluator should be able to analyze software and evaluate its quality. A checklist (presented in Chapter Eleven) can be used to record judgments made while using the program and helps ensure that all areas are considered.

If an instructional management section is included in a particular program, it should also be evaluated. After gaining access to the section, the evaluator should investigate data handling and storage capabilities. Instructions for using this section should be clear and uncomplicated. The data collection should be useful to teachers and media specialists. This section should be capable of presenting instructors with all necessary information, and should not leave out any important data. For example, students' final test scores may not contain enough information to diagnose students' problems; therefore, a record of specific questions or types of questions which were answered incorrectly would be necessary.

The evaluator should also refer to any written documentation. This can help identify other functions of the software, may give instructions for access to an instructional management section, and may suggest additional uses of the program. Good written documentation supplements and extends information on the disk.

Whenever possible, students should be observed using the software under consideration. This helps to verify the evaluator's impressions of the software and can identify problems an adult could overlook.

Large Programs

Some software is presented as a set of disks instead of a single disk. Although it may be impractical to do an in-depth analysis of every disk in a multidisk set, the procedure described above should be followed for at least one of the disks. In addition, the evaluator should determine, in terms of content, where the series begins and how far it goes, or to what level it advances. It also helps to discover the amount of overlap, if any, between disks. That is, does Lesson 14 review any of Lesson 13 before introducing new material? If the answer is yes, how much of the new disk is old material? If there is no review, is there a pretest? If not, does there need to be a review or a pretest? Answers to such questions can help evaluators gauge the overall structure of software which covers a series of disks.

Checklists

It can be somewhat difficult to form an opinion about a program without something to guide interaction with the software. A checklist or evaluation form, which can help ensure that no important areas are overlooked, can also be used to record reactions to the program immediately, instead of trying to recall details later.

If several people are examining the same programs, evaluation forms can be used to compare and tabulate different opinions and to guide discussion. This type of directed interaction could be useful in reaching a final decision about whether or not to purchase a program.

Summary

A. Identify Needs to Be Met by Software
B. Sources of Titles
   1. Professional literature of education, library and information science, and computer science
   2. Publishers' catalogs
   3. Professional meetings and conventions
   4. Professional colleagues
C. Obtaining Material for Preview
   1. Request preview copy from dealer or publisher
      a. Use letterhead stationery or approved purchase order
      b. State that school won't approve purchase without preview
      c. Guarantee that no copy will be made
   2. Use program at microcomputer software center
   3. Use program at exhibit at professional meeting
   4. Sales representative can bring copies
   5. Users' clubs may have copies
D. Examining Program
   1. Run program first, using only information on the screen
      a. To become familiar with program in general
      b. To identify obvious flaws
   2. Experiment with and test the program
      a. Give creative responses
      b. Give slow and/or incorrect answers
      c. Check for branching and random order in presentation of exercises
   3. Evaluate instructional management section
   4. Evaluate printed documentation and support materials
   5. Watch a student use the program
E. Additional Procedures for Multidisk Sets
   1. Identify where series begins and ends
   2. Determine amount of overlap between disks
F. Use Checklists to Guide and Record Evaluation

SELECTED SOURCES

Anderson, Eric. "Software Selection Considerations," *ACCESS: Microcomputers in Libraries* 2 (July 1982): 10–11.

Heath, Charles S. "Software Selection and Evaluation: A Personal Perspective," *School Psychology Review* 13 (Fall 1984): 473–77.

Heck, William P.; Jerry Johnson; and Robert J. Kansky. *Guidelines for Evaluating Computerized Instructional Materials*. Reston, Va.: National Council of Teachers of Mathematics, 1981.

"How to Find Good Software," *Electronic Learning* 2 (October 1982): 40–43.

Lathrop, Ann. "Microcomputer Courseware: Selection and Evaluation," *Top of the News* 39 (Spring 1983): 265–74.

Riesenberg, Bruce. "Selecting Computer Hardware and Software," *New Directions for Student Services* 7 (June 1984): 21–32.

Test, David W. "Evaluating Educational Software for the Microcomputer," *Journal of Special Education Technology* 7 (Summer 1985): 37–46.

10
Balancing Concerns

After a program has been previewed and analyzed, a decision must be made whether or not to purchase and use it. Inasmuch as nothing is perfect, the selection process becomes one of deciding whether a software's good points compensate for its weak points.

When *Not* to Purchase

It would not make sense to purchase a program that would never be used. In this case, even an excellent program would be a waste of money. High schools would have little or no need for software designed to teach the twenty-six letters of the alphabet. Elementary schools would probably not use a program to prepare students for the SAT. If it is possible to foresee that a program will not be used, it is not reasonable to spend money to buy it.

Nor is there any reason to buy software that will not work on the microcomputer equipment in one's school. Although many makes and models of microcomputers are available, software made for one microcomputer may not run on another—just as 8-track tapes won't work in a cassette player.

Besides make and model, there are other considerations. Software is sold on floppy disks, cassettes, or solid-state cartridges, and the type that is purchased must match the input devices on the available equipment. Each program requires a certain amount of storage space in the microcomputer in order to operate, and the needed amount is expressed as so many *K*s (16K, 48K, etc.). Make sure, then, that the capacity of the microcomputer is equal to (or greater than) the amount needed by the program.

Also, microcomputers are programmed in various "languages," and to run, a particular educational program must be written in a language "spoken" by the microcomputer. This also means that the program must be compatible with the program's operating system, often abbreviated as *DOS*.

Finally, some software requires "extra" devices in order to run or for the instructor or student to get the maximum use from it. These mandatory extras may include a second disk drive, a printer, game paddles, or a color monitor. If this is the case, the school should either have or be in the process of purchasing these items.

Documentation should state very clearly the equipment needed to run the program. If further equipment is needed, usually the producer or distributor of the software can identify its requirements and help the teacher or media specialist determine whether it is compatible with the available microcomputer hardware.

Another situation which would probably be cause for not purchasing an item is errors in the program. This includes incorrect spelling, grammatical and content mistakes, and problems in the way the program runs. For example, some poorly written software will crash, or simply stop, in the middle of the program while the user is following directions. Such sloppiness is not tolerated in other media, and should not be accepted in educational software either.

Serious but Less Critical Problems

The problems discussed above should probably be considered serious enough to overrule purchase of the software. Other problems, while serious, are somewhat less critical, and the teachers and media specialists must decide whether they are important enough to preclude purchase or are outweighed by positive factors.

Floppy disks, and to a certain extent other input devices, tend to be very fragile. Users are not always very careful, and sometimes there are equipment failures. Whatever the reason, a disk can be severely damaged very quickly. Many software producers and distributors either allow schools to make a backup copy of the program or will provide a replacement at nominal cost. If not, the replacement cost of damaged software can be a very critical consideration for expensive programs or for disks in a series, where a number of them are necessary to run the program. It is less of a problem with less expensive software.

The time needed to run a program may be a critical consideration. Like a Monopoly game, some software can run almost forever. If students can stop and resume play later, this is less of a problem. The specific situation in individual schools will be the determining factor.

The way a program responds to wrong answers needs to be carefully evaluated. It is best not to purchase software which addresses students in a derogatory manner. Likewise, it is wise to avoid programs which reward failure—like exploding a bomb after several wrong answers. Other types of poor responses to wrong answers are less critical. The evaluator should carefully examine and analyze responses to wrong answers to ensure that the program does not undermine a student's self-image or promote poor educational practice. Based on the results of this analysis, the teacher or media specialist may decide not to purchase or use the item.

The ability to turn the sound off in a program also needs to be considered. In this case, it is important to know where the program will be used. The factors to be considered are whether other students in the area will be disturbed and whether a particular program is liable to "announce" student errors. The amount and type of sound in the program are other considerations.

The cooperation and help available from the producer or distributor of software must also be considered. Software quality is of major importance, and unsuitable programs should probably not be purchased, but poor support from a vendor may, by itself, result in a decision not to purchase an otherwise worthwhile program or programs. A good vendor tries to satisfy his customer, and works to solve problems which may arise. Some will help teachers and school library media specialists who have trouble operating a program. Some will exchange software that is found to be unsuitable, or damaged disks may be replaced with new ones. Overall, if there is some difficulty with purchased software, good vendors make an effort to work with educators until a satisfactory solution is found.

Pragmatically, price and potential use are very important. An excellent but expensive program, which would be used only once a year, may be passed over in favor of several less expensive but good programs which could be used more often. It is now possible to buy a set of multiple copies of a single program for less than the total price of each one purchased individually. Often a disk works with only one microcomputer at a time, so these "labpacks" can be both useful and cost effective if heavy use is anticipated. It is now possible to have in-school *networks,* where one disk will run multiple microcomputers. If this is an anticipated use of software, permission must be obtained from the producer so that copyright regulations are not violated.

After one uses a checklist and evaluates a program, it is possible to scan the recorded information quickly. It may be wise to avoid purchasing or using those programs with more weaknesses than strengths. If a final decision will be based on the evaluation form, it is probably desirable to determine acceptable and unacceptable scores before programs are examined.

Final Decision

No software is perfect. Every item has strengths and weaknesses. It is the evaluator's job to identify those virtues and defects and then decide which outweigh the others. It is a judgment call. Educational professionals are trained in the identification and selection of materials that can help students learn. This expertise should be applied in the final decision whether or not to purchase and/or use a specific program, after a careful analysis of that program and its content within the framework of a school.

Summary

A. Reasons for *Not* Purchasing/Using
  1. Won't be used
  2. Won't work with available microcomputer equipment
  3. Mistakes in program
B. Problems Which May Be Serious Enough to Refuse Purchase/Use:
  1. Denial of backup copy
  2. Time needed to run the program
  3. How program responds to wrong answers
  4. Inability to turn off sound
  5. Price and predicted use
  6. Vendor support
  7. More weaknesses than strengths
C. Final Decision Is a Judgment Call and Should Be Based on Professional Expertise

SELECTED SOURCES

Heck, William P.; Jerry Johnson; and Robert J. Kansky. *Guidelines for Evaluating Computerized Instructional Materials.* Reston, Va.: National Council of Teachers of Mathematics, 1981.

Lathrop, Ann. "The Terrible Ten in Educational Programming: My Top Ten Reasons for Automatically Rejecting a Program," *Educational Computer Magazine* (September/October 1982): 34.

MicroSIFT. *Evaluator's Guide for Microcomputer-Based Instructional Packages.* Eugene: Dept. of Computer and Information Science, Univ. of Oregon, 1982.

11
Evaluation Checklist

I. When you receive an educational microcomputer software program to evaluate or preview, supply the following information as accurately and completely as possible.

A. Program title: _____

Series title (if applicable): _____

Local vendor: _____

_____

Cost: _____ Copyright date: _____

B. Hardware specifications and compatibility:

Make/model microcomputer: _____

Memory required: _____

Program language: _____

DOS: _____

Required peripherals:

_____ second disk drive   _____ color monitor

_____ graphics capabilities   _____ printer

_____ game paddles   _____ other (specify):

                                   _____

Input device: _____ cassette

_____ floppy disk   _____ cartridge

C. Subject/curriculum area: _____

   Age/grade level: _____

II. When considering a piece of instructional microcomputer software for purchase, answer the following questions.

		Yes	No
1.	Will this program run on my model of microcomputer?	___	___
2.	Does my microcomputer have enough memory capacity to run this program?	___	___
3.	Do I already have all the necessary extras to make this program run (e.g., second disk drive, printer, game paddles, color monitor)?	___	___
4.	Is this program written in a language my microcomputer "speaks"?	___	___
5.	Is the input device compatible with my equipment?	___	___
6.	Is a backup copy of this program readily available?	___	___
7.	Will this program be used in my school or library, instead of sitting on the shelf?	___	___
8.	Are there mistakes in this program? (This includes spelling, grammatical, content, and/or programming errors.)	___	___
9.	Will good vendor support be available after the program is purchased?	___	___

A negative response to any of the above should cause the reviewer or reviewers to seriously consider *not* purchasing the program.

III. Now run the program on the microcomputer and respond to the following statements. Try to run the program normally, without any deliberate mistakes. Then see how it responds to errors. While working with the program, indicate how much you agree with the following statements. Skip those statements which do not apply to the program being evaluated.

	Strongly Agree	Agree	Disagree	Strongly Disagree
A. Presentation of Content				
1. Program content is accurate.	___	___	___	___
2. Program is up to date or current.	___	___	___	___
3. Program is unbiased and free of stereotyping.	___	___	___	___

	Strongly Agree	Agree	Disagree	Strongly Disagree

4. Information is presented on computer screen in nonconfusing manner. ____ ____ ____ ____

5. Program is compatible with texts and other materials. ____ ____ ____ ____

B. Educational Quality

1. Authors have background or training in education. ____ ____ ____ ____

2. Program was pretested and revised. ____ ____ ____ ____

3. Possible to identify program goal(s) and objectives. ____ ____ ____ ____

4. Program enhances, supports, and supplements school objectives. ____ ____ ____ ____

5. Material organized in small, well-sequenced units. ____ ____ ____ ____

6. Information or skill presented more than once. ____ ____ ____ ____

7. Builds from familiar to the new or unknown. ____ ____ ____ ____

8. Required user response matches program objectives and/or desired type of learning. ____ ____ ____ ____

9. Required response matches skills of target audience. ____ ____ ____ ____

10. Program requirements match target audience. ____ ____ ____ ____

11. Reading level of program and its instructions match target audience. ____ ____ ____ ____

12. Prerequisite skills match both program and target audience. ____ ____ ____ ____

13. Where appropriate, computer screen is adapted for young users. ____ ____ ____ ____

	Strongly Agree	Agree	Disagree	Strongly Disagree

14. Neither content nor documentation is offensive or condescending to users. ____ ____ ____ ____

15. Program is suitable for type and amount of anticipated use. ____ ____ ____ ____

16. Intended user can work with program independently. ____ ____ ____ ____

C. Documentation and Support Materials

   1. Manual well constructed and understandable. ____ ____ ____ ____

   2. Manual discusses advantages, disadvantages, and unique features of program. ____ ____ ____ ____

   3. Manual uses good organizational aids. ____ ____ ____ ____

   4. Manual gives clear directions on access to and use of instructional management portions of program. ____ ____ ____ ____

   5. Program can be used by following only directions which appear on computer screen. ____ ____ ____ ____

   6. On-screen instructions are clear, concise, and easy to follow. ____ ____ ____ ____

   7. Experienced users can bypass on-screen beginners' instructions. ____ ____ ____ ____

   8. Support materials do more than duplicate program content. ____ ____ ____ ____

   9. Support materials are educationally sound. ____ ____ ____ ____

10. Program and accompanying materials are self-contained. ____ ____ ____ ____

	Strongly Agree	Agree	Disagree	Strongly Disagree

D. User Interaction with Program and Operating Interaction

    1. User controls pace of program and, where appropriate, its direction. ____ ____ ____ ____

    2. Frequent opportunities for user interaction. ____ ____ ____ ____

    3. Function assigned particular key is consistent throughout program. ____ ____ ____ ____

    4. User can correct mistakes while entering information. ____ ____ ____ ____

Response to Correct Answers

    5. Program acknowledges and/or rewards correct answers. ____ ____ ____ ____

    6. Variety in rewards for correct answers. ____ ____ ____ ____

Response to Content Errors

    7. Program gives users second chance and/or repeats pertinent part of program. ____ ____ ____ ____

    8. Program does not simply indicate answer is wrong and then continues. ____ ____ ____ ____

    9. Program does not respond to wrong answers with insulting or derogatory messages. ____ ____ ____ ____

    10. Program does not use flashy, elaborate response to wrong answers. ____ ____ ____ ____

    11. No audible response to wrong answers. ____ ____ ____ ____

Response to Format Errors

    12. Program prompts user when incorrect command is given. ____ ____ ____ ____

    13. Program prompts user when answer does not match required format or given list. ____ ____ ____ ____

	Strongly Agree	Agree	Disagree	Strongly Disagree

14. Program accepts minor misspellings, where appropriate. ____ ____ ____ ____

E. Utilization of Microcomputer Strengths

1. Program branches; i.e., user response determines subsequent questions or information. ____ ____ ____ ____

2. Program is more than computerized workbook. ____ ____ ____ ____

3. Program gives immediate feedback. ____ ____ ____ ____

4. Problems presented in random order. ____ ____ ____ ____

5. Screen display well designed and uncluttered. ____ ____ ____ ____

6. Graphics are distinct, understandable, and well designed. ____ ____ ____ ____

7. Graphics highlight or emphasize key points. ____ ____ ____ ____

8. Color or shading is used effectively. ____ ____ ____ ____

9. Sound is used appropriately (e.g., to reward correct answer, enhance instruction, give directions). ____ ____ ____ ____

10. It is easy to turn off sound. ____ ____ ____ ____

F. Instructional Management

1. Program records responses of individual users. ____ ____ ____ ____

2. Program can store scores of more than one user. ____ ____ ____ ____

3. Program differentiates between right answers on first, second, third try, etc. ____ ____ ____ ____

	Strongly Agree	Agree	Disagree	Strongly Disagree
4. Program identifies type(s) of problems that gives a student difficulty.	____	____	____	____
5. Program gives initial diagnosis of student strengths and weaknesses.	____	____	____	____
6. Instructional management section is easy to use.	____	____	____	____
7. Possible for teacher or librarian to tailor program to users.	____	____	____	____
8. Possible to print out information in instructional management section.	____	____	____	____
9. Instructional management section has procedures to protect its information.	____	____	____	____

IV. In addition to the general statements in Section III, there are considerations which pertain to specific formats. Respond to statements in the following categories appropriate to the program being evaluated. Skip sections or statements which do not apply.

	Strongly Agree	Agree	Disagree	Strongly Disagree
A. Drill and Practice Programs				
1. Program is repetitious.	____	____	____	____
2. Program has progressive levels of difficulty.	____	____	____	____
B. Tutorial Programs				
1. Assume some of the task of instruction.	____	____	____	____
2. Frequently assess user performance.	____	____	____	____
C. Problem-solving Programs				
1. User input influences situation presented.	____	____	____	____

	Strongly Agree	Agree	Disagree	Strongly Disagree
2. Program reacts to each user action.	___	___	___	___
3. Program contains all relevant details.	___	___	___	___
4. Program responds to wide variety of user actions.	___	___	___	___

D. Games/Simulations

	Strongly Agree	Agree	Disagree	Strongly Disagree
1. Program has varying and progressive levels of difficulty.	___	___	___	___
2. User responses, not chance alone, determine results of program.	___	___	___	___
3. User can stop and return to program later without penalty.	___	___	___	___
4. Games are fun to play.	___	___	___	___
5. Simulations include all essential elements of real situation and interrelationships among these elements are accurate.	___	___	___	___

E. Shell Programs

	Strongly Agree	Agree	Disagree	Strongly Disagree
1. Program has simple procedure for changing content.	___	___	___	___
2. Program accepts both letters and numbers.	___	___	___	___

V. The next step is to obtain an overall rating for the program being evaluated. To do this, count the total number of statements you *strongly agree* with, the number you *agree* with, the number you *disagree* with, and the number you *strongly disagree* with; and fill in the blanks below.

Strongly Agree	Agree	Disagree	Strongly Disagree
_____	_____	_____	_____

The sum of the numbers in the first two blanks (*strongly agree* and *agree*) is the total number of criteria on which the program was marked favorably or on which it performed well. The sum of the last two numbers (*disagree* and *strongly disagree*) indicates the total number of evaluative criteria where the program does not perform well. These two figures summarize your reaction to the program and represent the number of its strengths (*strongly agree* and *agree*) and the number of its weaknesses (*disagree* and *strongly disagree*).

The numbers which result from this method should not be used as absolute guidelines. Instead, they provide a quick summary of your reaction and can help you come to a final decision. It is possible for a useful program to have a few more weaknesses than strengths, and you may wish to use or purchase such a program. It is also possible for a program to have a few more strengths than weaknesses, but the identified weaknesses may be more important than the strengths. In this case, the decision may be not to purchase or use the program.

VI. The last step is to make a final decision. Remember that no program is perfect. Then, based on the information gathered, use your professional judgment to determine whether or not to recommend this program.

_____ 1. I recommend this program for purchase or use.

_____ 2. I recommend this program with reservations or stipulations. (Please specify.)

_____

_____

_____

_____

_____

_____ 3. I do not recommend this program for either purchase or use.

Program Title: _____

Evaluator's Name: _____

Date: _____

Glossary

Back Up Copy. Replica of original program, used to replace disks, cassettes, or cartridges which are severely damaged or destroyed.

Branching Program. Program where next question or sequence of information is determined by user response to current questions.

Computer-Assisted Instruction (CAI). Integration of computer and corresponding software into the educational process to supplement (not replace) the teacher.

Crash. Occurs when program stops running before it reaches the end.

Cursor. Marker (often a flashing square or bar) which indicates place on monitor where typed information will appear.

Disk. Round, flat surface, covered with magnetic material, on which data can be stored. **Floppy disks**, usually 5-1/4 inches across and flexible, are most often used for educational software.

Documentation. Information about a program and its use. Can be either in printed form or contained within the program.

Drill and Practice Program. Provides students repetitious exercises on material or facts already presented by teacher or school library media specialist.

Educational Software. Program specifically designed to teach or help teach something. May enhance, supplement, or support the instructional process.

Feedback. Responses made by microcomputer to users' answers or questions.

Floppy Disk. See **Disk**.

Game. Contest based on skills and/or chance that is played according to rules.

Green Screen. Microcomputer monitor that does not have color capabilities; therefore all letters, numbers, and graphics are green.

Input. Information, answers, or directions entered into microcomputer—i.e., what user tells the machine.

Input Device. Floppy disk, cassette, or solid-state cartridge which contains a program and transfers all or part of that program into the microcomputer.

Instructional Management Section. Portion of program which assumes some of the instructional tasks for teachers and school library media specialists. It may gather and record data on student performance and/or allow teacher control of the type, number, and level of questions or information given to specific users.

Instructional Software. See **Educational Software**.

Linear Program. Program where every user answers every question in the same sequence: question 1 to question 2 to question 3, and so on.

Menu. Program's table of contents or directory. Is included in program itself, and can be read from the microcomputer monitor.

Monitor. Video screen connected to a computer. Prints information on its screen as it communicates with user, displaying both machine messages and user responses or input.

Packaging. Box, envelope, binder, etc. which contains disk, cassette, or cartridge with program and any accompanying materials.

Printout. Paper copy of information generated by the microcomputer.

Problem-Solving Program. User applies learning or knowledge already possessed to determine answer or solution to the information or situation presented.

Program. Set of instructions which tells the microcomputer what to do and how to respond to or handle the information it is given.

Screen. See **Monitor**.

Shell Program. Program where, within a given structure, information or questions (on almost any topic) can be put in by teacher or school library media specialist.

Simulation. Program designed to represent real-life activities by providing essential elements of real situation.

Software. That information which is inside, or put inside, the microcomputer. Three types are (1) language and information built into machine and a permanent part of it; (2) program put into machine which causes it to perform in specific manner (which is the focus of this book); and (3) information or data put in by user while working with a program.

Support Materials. Worksheets, suggested activities, or other supplemental items which accompany software.

Target Audience. Children or young adults who are the intended users of a program or a piece of software.

Tutorial Program. Assumes some of the task of teaching, so that student needs only minimal instruction before using the program.

Vendor. Producer, dealer, or distributor who sells microcomputer software or programs.

Bibliography

Ahl, David H. "Selecting and Buying Educational Software," in *Creative Computing 1983 Software Buyer's Guide*. Morris Plains, N.J.: Ahl Publishing Co., pp. 24–28.

American Library Association. American Association of School Librarians and Association for Educational Communications and Technology. *Media Programs: District and School*. Chicago: American Library Assn., 1975.

Anderson, Eric. "Software Selection Considerations," *ACCESS: Microcomputers in Libraries* 2 (July 1982): 10–11.

Bland, Barbara B. "Evaluation: The Key to Selecting Quality Microcomputer Courseware for School Media Collections," *North Carolina Libraries* 40 (Fall/Winter 1982): 191–97 + .

Brown, James W.; Richard B. Lewis; and Fred F. Harcleroad. *AV Instruction: Technology, Media and Methods*. 6th ed. New York: McGraw-Hill, 1983.

Chan, Julie M. T. "The Promise of Computers for Reluctant Readers," *School Library Journal* 32 (November 1985): 120–30.

Coburn, Peter, et al. *Practical Guide to Computers in Education* (2nd ed.). Reading, Mass.: Addison-Wesley, 1985.

Cohen, Vicki Blum. "Criteria for the Evaluation of Microcomputer Courseware," *Educational Technology* 23 (January 1983): 9–14.

————. "What Is Instructionally Effective Microcomputer Software?" *Viewpoints in Teaching and Learning* 59 (Spring 1983); 13–27.

Collopy, David. "Software Documentation: Reading a Package by Its Cover," *Personal Computing* 7 (February 1983); 134–44.

Daetz, Denney. "Bellwether Social Studies Programs," *Classroom Computer Learning* 6 (November/December 1985): 46–47 + .

Dyer, Susan R., and Richard C. Forcier. "How to Pick Computer Software," *Instructional Innovator* 27 (September 1982): 38–40.

Eldredge, Bruce, and Kenneth Delp. "How to Evaluate Educational Computer Programs," *Media & Methods* 17 (March 1981): 4 + .

Gallagher, Francine L. "What Educators Want in Microcomputer Software," *Catholic Library World* 55 (February 1984): 290–93.

Hakes, Barbara. "Selecting Microcomputer Software," *Wyoming Library Roundup* 39 (Spring/Summer 1984): 46–48.

Bibliography

Harper, Dennis O., and James H. Stewart, eds. *Run: Computer Education* (2nd ed.). Monterey, Calif.: Brooks/Cole, 1986.

Heath, Charles S. "Software Selection and Evaluation: A Personal Perspective," *School Psychology Review* 13 (Fall 1984): 473–77.

Heck, William P.; Jerry Johnson; and Robert J. Kansky. *Guidelines for Evaluating Computerized Instructional Materials.* Reston, Va.: National Council of Teachers of Mathematics, 1981.

"How to Find Good Software," *Electronic Learning* 2 (October 1982): 40–43.

"How to Select Software for Kids," *Instructor* 94 (October 1984): 90.

Keogh, James Edward. "The Classroom Crystal Ball," *Microcomputing* 6 (February 1982): 94–98.

Kepner, Henry S., ed. *Computers in the Classroom.* Washington, D.C.: National Education Assn., 1982.

Kingman, James C. "Designing Good Educational Software," *Creative Computing* 7 (October 1981): 72–81.

Kleiman, Glenn M. *Brave New Schools: How Computers Can Change Education.* Reston, Va.: Reston Publishing Co., 1984.

_____; Mary M. Humphrey; and Trudy Van Buskirk. "Evaluating Educational Software," *Creative Computing* 7 (October 1981): 84–90.

Krause, Kenneth C. "Choosing Computer Software That Works," *Journal of Reading* 28 (October 1984): 24–27.

Lathrop, Ann. "Microcomputer Courseware: Selection and Evaluation," *Top of the News* 39 (Spring 1983): 265–74.

_____. "The Terrible Ten in Educational Programming: My Top Ten Reasons for Automatically Rejecting a Program," *Educational Computer Magazine* (September/October 1982): 34.

Littlefield, Patti. "Pointers for Parents Looking for Educational Software," *Infoworld* 5 (1983): 17.

MicroSIFT. *Evaluator's Guide for Microcomputer-Based Instructional Packages.* Eugene: Dept. of Computer and Information Science, Univ. of Oregon, 1982.

Olds, Henry F. "Evaluating Written Guides to Software," *Classroom Computer News* 2 (November/December 1982): 54.

Piestrup, Ann. "What Makes Superior Educational Software?" *Compute!'s Apple Applications* 1 (Spring/Summer 1985): 47–51.

Raleigh, C. Patrick. "Give Your Child a Head Start," *Personal Software* 1 (November 1983): 36–53.

Riesenberg, Bruce. "Selecting Computer Hardware and Software," *New Directions for Student Services* 7 (June 1984): 21–32.

Riordin, Tim. "How to Select Software You Can Trust," *Classroom Computer News* 3 (March 1983): 56–61.

Roberts, Nancy. "Testing the World with Simulations: When the Computer Is the Laboratory, the Subject Can Be Almost Anything," *Classroom Computer News* 3 (January/February 1983): 28–31.

74

Test, David W. "Evaluating Educational Software for the Microcomputer," *Journal of Special Education Technology* 7 (Summer 1985): 37–46.

Truett, Carol, and Lori Gillespie. *Choosing Educational Software: A Buyer's Guide.* Littleton, Colo.: Libraries Unlimited, 1984.

Watt, Molly. "Making a Case for Software Evaluation," *Computing Teacher* 10 (May 1982): 20–22.

Woolls, Blanche. "Selecting Microcomputer Software for the Library," *Top of the News* 39 (Summer 1983): 321–27.

Index

Index

Carol A. Doll is an associate professor in the College of Library and Information Science at the University of South Carolina. She has worked as a teacher and school librarian and is an active member of ALA, the South Carolina Library Association, and the South Carolina Association of School Librarians. Doll is the author of several articles on children's collections in school and public libraries and an article in *School Library Journal*, "The Care and Handling of Micro Disks."